Diversity and Inclusion in Libraries

Medical Library Association Books

The Medical Library Association (MLA) features books that showcase the expertise of health sciences librarians for other librarians and professionals.

MLA Books are excellent resources for librarians in hospitals, medical research practice, and other settings. These volumes will provide health care professionals and patients with accurate information that can improve outcomes and save lives.

Each book in the series has been overseen editorially since conception by the Medical Library Association Books Panel, composed of MLA members with expertise spanning the breadth of health sciences librarianship.

Medical Library Association Books Panel

Kristen L. Young, AHIP, chair
Dorothy Ogdon, AHIP, chair designate
Michel C. Atlas
Carolann Lee Curry
Kelsey Leonard, AHIP
Karen McElfresh, AHIP
JoLinda L. Thompson, AHIP
Heidi Heilemann, AHIP, board liaison

About the Medical Library Association

Founded in 1898, MLA is a 501(c)(3) nonprofit, educational organization of 3,500 individual and institutional members in the health sciences information field that provides lifelong educational opportunities, supports a knowledgebase of health information research, and works with a global network of partners to promote the importance of quality information for improved health to the health care community and the public.

Books in the Series

The Medical Library Association Guide to Providing Consumer and Patient Health Information, edited by Michele Spatz
Health Sciences Librarianship, edited by M. Sandra Wood
Curriculum-Based Library Instruction: From Cultivating Faculty Relationships to Assessment, edited by Amy Blevins and Megan Inman
The Small Library Manager's Handbook, by Alice Graves
Mobile Technologies for Every Library, by Ann Whitney Gleason
The Medical Library Association Guide to Answering Questions about the Affordable Care Act, edited by Emily Vardell

Diversity and Inclusion in Libraries

*A Call to Action and
Strategies for Success*

Edited by
Shannon D. Jones
Beverly Murphy

ROWMAN & LITTLEFIELD
Lanham • Boulder • New York • London

Published by Rowman & Littlefield
An imprint of The Rowman & Littlefield Publishing Group, Inc.
4501 Forbes Boulevard, Suite 200, Lanham, Maryland 20706
www.rowman.com

6 Tinworth Street, London SE11 5AL

British Library Cataloguing in Publication Information Available

Library of Congress Cataloging-in-Publication Data

Names: Jones, Shannon D., 1974- editor. | Murphy, Beverly, 1957- editor.
Title: Diversity and inclusion in libraries : a call to action and strategies for success / edited by
    Shannon D. Jones, Beverly Murphy.
Description: Lanham : Rowman & Littlefield, [2019] | Series: Medical Library Association Books |
    Includes bibliographical references and index.
Identifiers: LCCN 2019010814 (print) | LCCN 2019012444 (ebook) | ISBN 9781538114407 (elec-
    tronic) | ISBN 9781538114384 (cloth : alk. paper) | ISBN 9781538114391 (pbk. : alk. paper)
Subjects: LCSH: Minorities in library science—United States. | Minority librarians—United States. |
    Diversity in the workplace—United States. | Libraries and minorities—United States. | Medical
    libraries—United States—Employees.
Classification: LCC Z682.4.M56 (ebook) | LCC Z682.4.M56 D577 2019 (print) | DDC 023/.9—dc23
LC record available at https://lccn.loc.gov/2019010814

Printed in the United States of America

Contents

Preface

Libraries today are faced not only with acquiring, teaching, collecting, pre-serving, and distributing information to their patrons but also with issues of diversity and inclusion within their staff and the patrons they serve. By the year 2050, close to 50% of the U.S. population will be comprised of people of color (Broughton, 2008). In a recent study of public library staff and future librarians, Mary E. Brown found participants agreed that library staff should represent the diversity of the communities served; there was little support, however, for actively attempting to advance proportional representation through education or hiring (Brown, 2015).

Our rationale for serving as editors of this book is multifaceted and far reaching. As women of color, we share a common interest in diversity and inclusion issues and have worked diligently through networking, mentoring, workshops, and personal bonding to bring underrepresented populations into the library profession and particularly into medical librarianship. "It is no secret that librarianship has traditionally been and continues to be a profes-sion dominated by whiteness (Bourg, 2014; Branche, 2012; Galvan, 2015; Hall, 2012; Honma, 2006), which is a theoretical concept that can extend beyond the realities of racial privilege to a wide range of dominant ideologies based on gender identity, sexual orientation, class, and other categories" (Hathcock, 2015). Though many libraries alike *talk the talk* when it comes to embracing and supporting diversity and inclusion initiatives, they often fall short when it comes to *walking the walk*. We would like to see diversity and inclusion be not just a trendy topic of discussion but also a process of action supported by effective, best-practice strategies and tempered by experiences and wisdom. We hope this book will help in this effort and be uniquely equipped to provide such a catalyst.

Both the news and scholarly literature are replete with information describing challenges that individuals from diverse backgrounds face in the workplace every day. This book explores some of the challenges that libraries and librarians face due to diversity and inclusion issues among library staff, as well as the patrons whom they serve. The primary goal of this compilation is to increase awareness of and sensitivity to the social, cultural, and educational needs of everyone involved. This publication should appeal to a broad audience whose interest is in diversity as it relates to libraries and librarianship, including professional librarians and paraprofessional library staff. Developing curriculums for library science students will not be a primary focus, though library science faculties may find the content of interest. *Diversity and Inclusion in Libraries* is divided into three parts: "Why Diversity and Inclusion Matter," "Equipping the Library Staff," and "Voices From the Field."

Part 1 explores the role diversity and inclusion have played in librarianship, addressing the question of its importance and relevance. Within this section, Chapter 1 offers a historical perspective of African Americans in librarianship, Chapter 2 provides an overview of diversity and inclusion literature and research, Chapter 3 examines the changing face of librarianship, Chapter 4 discusses implicit bias and microaggressions in libraries, and Chapter 5 concentrates on social justice and activism in libraries.

In Part 2, authors share experiences, lessons learned, practical strategies, and challenges faced when building a library staff who is not only diverse but also equipped with the knowledge and experiences needed to serve a diverse clientele. The central theme addressed in this section is how to prepare the library staff to work with the array of diversity issues common in workplaces today. Chapter 6 showcases strategies for leading a diverse and inclusive public library. Chapter 7 discusses how to align a library's strategy with the parent organization's strategy. Chapter 8 focuses on recruiting and retaining a diverse workforce. Chapter 9 offers guidance on developing cultural competency and sensitivity. Chapter 10 examines professional development as a growth strategy.

Part 3 features the voices of diverse professionals who describe their experiences with diversity and inclusion issues in their respective environments. The section begins with Voice 1, where the author offers firsthand experience in writing and implementing diversity plans, recruiting underrepresented minorities (including LGBTQ librarians), and mentoring junior faculty in career advancement and tenure and promotion strategies. Part 3 concludes with Voice 10, where the author makes recommendations for improving communication and cultural humility among colleagues in medical education settings. Nestled between these voices, the authors share their candid experiences with disability and workplace accommodations; improving services for transgender students, faculties, and staff; recruiting Latinx and Native American graduate students into the librarianship pipeline; interpersonal relationships between minority women in leadership positions; being an African American male in health sciences librarianship or being an "other" in public librarianship; and creating a diversity committee.

Social media, movies, television, magazines, and so forth have not always been kind to the librarian. Our negative portrayal in films has ranged from the dowdy old maid in *It's a Wonderful Life* (Capra & Stewart, 1946) to the free-spirited club-hopper in *Party Girl* (Mayer et al., 1995). Stereotypical images abound about who we are and what we do, and it does not seem to be lessening, though Megan Rudolph states in her 2008 dissertation, "There is some evidence that the image of the librarian in film has begun to change" (p. 22). Rudolph (2008) also cites that a previous dissertation study by William King in 1990 "found that while individual librarian characters have changed over the years, the depiction of the profession as a whole has remained constant, which continues to reinforce the librarian stereotype" (p. 8).

"False perceptions and 'feminization' of the library profession" have resulted due to gender stereotypes that extend beyond the pay gap and leadership bias (Mars, 2018). Though male librarians are not immune to stereotyping, most of the stereotypical images of librarians portray White women, usually clad in a bun, with glasses, conservatively dressed, and reading or holding or book. Though we are the gatekeepers for knowledge, this is not at all how we should be portrayed. Even worse, librarians of color are rarely represented in popular culture, an image that doesn't lend itself to the younger generation. We must dispel the stereotypes especially in the underrepresented communities because they often don't see us represented in their environments, and when they do see us in that role, it is a negatively associated connation.

Often, we as librarians perpetuate these stereotypes in jest, not helping society get a clearer picture of who we are. We need to be sure to present ourselves and our profession in an engaging and attractive way to ensure that the younger generation sees librarianship as a viable career option. There is an African proverb that says it takes a village to raise a child. We believe the same is true for cultivating and nurturing future information professionals. We must reach the youngest generation (middle school, high school, etc.) because they are our potential pool of the next generation of librarians, and that will be different from what we are now.

Diversity and Inclusion in Libraries is a call to action for libraries to be proactive and intentional promoters and receivers of diversity and inclusion. Libraries and librarians alike can no longer afford to be silent or passive participants. As noted by Katherine Phillips, "Being around people who are different from us makes us more creative, more diligent and harder-working" (2014). It is our collective responsibility to create opportunities where individuals are encouraged and supported to bring their most authentic selves to the table. We should create environments where individuals feel free to use whichever personal pronouns suit them, where transgender patrons and staff members feel safe and comfortable to use the restroom of their choice, where minority librarians and staff members are offered the same support and development as their White counterparts, where minority personnel are able to bring their voices and lived experiences to discussions without being attacked or accused of making their White counterparts uncomfortable, and where barriers that may prevent people with disabilities from taking full advantage of library services and spaces are removed.

The concepts of diversity *and* inclusion should come as a package deal and not be mutually exclusive. As Verna Myers has argued, "Diversity is being invited to the party; inclusion is being asked to dance" (Cho, 2016). The journey toward creating libraries that are diverse and inclusive may not be an easy task, but it should be embraced and valued. We invite you to join us on this journey and use this collection of essays not only to increase your personal knowledge, understanding, and appreciation of diversity and inclusion but also more importantly to strengthen those efforts undertaken at your library. We hope this book will inspire you to take action, to acknowledge the beauty in our differences, and to embrace the concept that all voices matter. The communities we serve and are a part of depend on us getting this right.

REFERENCES

Broughton, A. (2008). Minorities expected to be majority in 2050. Retrieved from http://www.cnn.com/2008/US/08/13/census.minorities/

Brown, M. E. (2015). Invisible debility: Attitudes toward the underrepresented in library workplaces. *Public Library Quarterly, 34*(2), 124–133. doi:10.1080/01616846.2015.1036707

Capra, F., & Stewart, J. (1946). *It's a wonderful life* [Motion picture]. Los Angeles, CA: Liberty Films.

Cho, J. H. (2016). Diversity is being invited to the party; inclusion is being asked to dance, Verna Myers tells Cleveland bar. Retrieved from http://www.cleveland.com/business/index.ssf/2016/05/diversity_is_being_invited_to.html

Hathcock, A. (2015). White librarianship in blackface: Diversity initiatives in LIS. *In the Library With the Lead Pipe.* Retrieved from http://www.inthelibrarywiththeleadpipe.org/2015/lis-diversity/

Mars, P. (2018). Gender demographics and perception in librarianship. Retrieved from http://scholarworks.sjsu.edu/slissrj/vol7/iss2/3

Mayer, D. S., Birckmayer, H., Posey, P., De, S. A., Díaz, G., Mitchell, D., & Schreiber, L. (1995). *Party girl* [Motion picture]. N.p.: Party Productions.

Phillips, K. (2014). How diversity makes us smarter. Retrieved from https://www.scientificamerican.com/article/how-diversity-makes-us-smarter/

Rudolph, M. (2008). Librarians in film: A changing stereotype [Master's thesis]. Retrieved from https://ils.unc.edu/MSpapers/3413.pdf

Acknowledgments

No one who achieves success does so without acknowledging the help of others. The wise and confident acknowledge this help with gratitude.
—Alfred North Whitehead

There is no way a compilation such as this could come to fruition without the support of the many people who make up our village:

To our significant others, Jerome Ballew and William Barnes, we appreciate your patience, understanding, and support throughout the entirety of this project. This project was a labor in love, and you were with us every step of the way. You not only bore the brunt of our frustrations but also celebrated each milestone we surpassed. We would not have been able to pull this off without you both standing in our corners.

To our mothers, Suretha Jones, Joyce English, and Helen Holt, who are no longer with us but are still here in spirit. We love you, and we miss you. Thank you for being our strong African American women role models and for raising us to know we could do and be whatever we wanted in life as long as we work hard, are honest and fair, keep God in our lives, and be ourselves.

To our tribe, the African American Medical Librarians Alliance (AAM-LA) SIG of the Medical Library Association, we extend a heartfelt thanks for loving, encouraging, and supporting us. We appreciate your service as trusted advisors and confidants when being a librarian of color in White spaces was taking its toll on us mentally and physically. Lastly, a heartfelt thank-you for rallying around us when we decided to take on this project. We are so very proud to stand among you as colleagues.

To Jordan Wrigley, Duke University Medical Center Library and Archives, words cannot express how much we appreciate your prowess with the APA writing style and formatting. We could not have bought this project to completion without your help. Many thanks to you.

To the staff of the Duke University Medical Center Library and Archives, thank you so much for your support.

To Lisa Kerr, Medical University of South Carolina, for offering feedback on early drafts as we worked through the proposal phase of this project. Thank you so much for helping us get off to an excellent start.

To the staff of the Medical University of South Carolina Libraries, whom I am so proud to work among as well as serve as your leader. I am grateful for the opportunity to lead such a great group of individuals. Thanks for being an *amazing* team who makes the library run like a well-oiled machine. I appreciate your collective commitment and effort to make our library a place where patrons and staff alike come to do their best work. Thank you.

To our contributors, we appreciate your willingness to take this journey with us and add your voice to this important work. More importantly, thank you for helping to raise awareness about diversity and inclusion issues that are occurring in libraries today. There is still much work to be done to diversify the library workforce and provide spaces that are inclusive, welcoming, and safe for all. Thank you for being brave, having the courage to tell authentic and meaningful stories, and encouraging readers to think about the role they might play in making diverse experiences better in their respective libraries. Your stories touched us, and we are confident that they will be just as impactful for our readers.

Finally, we thank the readers of this compilation. We hope that you will keep an open mind and heart as you read each chapter.

Introduction

Chris Bourg

At a time when worries about race relations are at an all-time high (Swift, 2017), when women's marches and the #MeToo movement have pushed gender issues to the front of our national consciousness, and when the rights of people from marginalized communities are under threat, many are looking to public institutions like libraries to provide some mythical neutral space where differences are irrelevant and where "all sides" are welcomed and represented. Although I have argued elsewhere that libraries might in fact be ideally situated to provide inclusive, welcoming spaces where people can wrestle, individually or collectively, with controversial and divisive topics and with credible sources of insight and data about those topics (Bourg, 2016), I've also argued that libraries can never be neutral (Bourg, 2018). There is no doubt that libraries are vital and trusted social institutions. As the chapters in this book illustrate, however, libraries and those of us who work in them continue to have significant work to do to live up to the value of diversity and inclusion we espouse individually and collectively.

The arguably naïve view of libraries in the United States as safe havens from the current national environment of political polarization, rising xenophobia, emboldened White supremacy, and a backlash against queer people and other marginalized communities is easy to understand. Two recent and highly visible examples of libraries providing vital services to communities in the midst of heightened racial tensions include the Ferguson Municipal Library in 2014 and the Enoch Pratt Free Library in Baltimore in 2015. Following the protests in Ferguson over the killing of Michael Brown Jr., an 18-year-old Black male, and the grand jury's decision not to charge the police officer who killed him, the Ferguson Municipal Library stayed open and provided a gathering place and other resources for the community (Cleveland, 2015). Similarly, the CEO of the Enoch Pratt Free Library in

Baltimore, Dr. Carla Hayden, now librarian of Congress, kept the library open throughout weeks of unrest and protests after Freddie Gray Jr., a 25-year-old Black male, died while in police custody. Hayden described the library as "the community's anchor. It's the heart of the community at good times and bad times" (Cotrell, 2015).

Members of the library community who work in libraries of all kinds across the country create guides, programs, and book displays promoting diversity, inclusion, and social justice; hold and attend conferences about diversity; and participate formally and informally in all manner of activities in support of a more diverse and inclusive profession. The visibility of all these efforts on social media has even led some misguided observers to declare, with no evidence, that "many university librarians are left-wing zealots . . . [who] spend large parts of their days on Twitter, advocating for social justice causes, signalling virtue by retweeting hate speech directed at Donald Trump" (Beall, 2019).

The hard reality is that, when it comes to diversity and inclusion, libraries are neither the idealized, safe, neutral, all-inclusive havens many of our wishful-thinking fans imagine we are nor the cesspools of social justice run amok, led by rabid left-wing zealots, as some or our detractors accuse us of being. The truth is that libraries are overwhelmingly White—not just demographically but culturally as well. As Hathcock explains, the cultural whiteness of American libraries and librarianship "is a theoretical concept that can extend beyond the realities of racial privilege to a wide range of dominant ideologies based on gender identity, sexual orientation, class, and other categories" (2015).

In fact, I am writing this introduction in the immediate aftermath of the 2019 American Library Association (ALA) midwinter meeting, where many marginalized people experienced racist, sexist, ableist, and antitransgender attitudes and behaviors. Perhaps the most public incident involved my friend and colleague and one of the few Black women on the ALA Council, April Hathcock, who was verbally attacked by a fellow council member during a council forum. The values of our profession notwithstanding, no one present stood up to her abuser, a White man, nor stepped up at the moment to support her (Hathcock, 2019; McKenzie, 2019). The ALA executive board issued a statement offering apologies to Hathcock and to others who experienced violations of the ALA Code of Conduct and promised to put processes and training in place to make all ALA events and spaces safer for everyone (ALA Member News, 2019). While our associations, our individual libraries, and perhaps most of our colleagues proclaim a heartfelt allegiance to the values of diversity and inclusion, and though many individuals and organizations are working hard to promote those values in their work, this example and too many others make it clear that we continue to fall painfully short in multiple ways.

The chapters in this volume provide answers to why diversity and inclusion matter in libraries, reveal strategies and examples to equip staff in libraries to lead and support diversity and inclusion efforts, and offer candid first-person accounts of individuals' experiences fighting for inclusive policies or simply fighting to be included and valued in their own workplaces and in the profession. In accepting the invitation to write the introduction to this book, I wrestled with the fact that I am a White woman (albeit a queer one), writing about diversity and inclusion in a profession that is dominated—demographically and culturally—by White women like me. My multiple intersecting identities as a director of an elite academic library; as a queer, White, cis-gendered woman; and as someone with degrees from prestigious institutions but/and with parents who did not attend college absolutely influence my views on and my experiences with diversity and inclusion in libraries, and in life. Although my whiteness and other privileges do not fully insulate me from backlash and trolling (McKenzie, 2018), White supremacist norms do grant me some unearned privilege to speak and write about the topics of diversity and inclusion and be heard by an audience that includes those not accustomed to listening to colleagues outside their typically homogeneous networks. It is my hope and my intention that lending my voice to this volume serves to amplify the voices within it and draws attention to the work we all need to do to make progress on diversity and inclusion and bring us closer to truly unlocking the liberatory potential of libraries.

REFERENCES

ALA Member News. (2019). ALA executive board releases statement regarding incident at council forum. Retrieved from http://www.ala.org/news/member-news/2019/01/ala-execu tive-board-releases-statement-regarding-incident-council-forum

Beall, J. (2019). Glamorised study halls do not need an army of librarians. Retrieved from https://www.timeshighereducation.com/opinion/glamorised-study-halls-do-not-need-army-librarians

Bourg, C. (2016). Libraries and the future of higher education. Retrieved from https://chris bourg.wordpress.com/2016/10/28/educause-2016-libraries-and-future-of-higher-education/

Bourg, C. (2018). Debating y/our humanity, or are libraries neutral. Retrieved from https://chrisbourg.wordpress.com/2018/02/11/debating-y-our-humanity-or-are-libraries-neutral/

Cleveland, L. (2015). "Library of the year" goes to Ferguson for efforts during protests. Retrieved from https://www.cnn.com/2015/06/10/us/ferguson-library-award/index.html

Cotrell, M. (2015). Baltimore's library stays open during unrest. Retrieved from https://americanlibrariesmagazine.org/blogs/the-scoop/qa-carla-hayden-baltimore/

Hathcock, A. (2015). White librarianship in blackface. Retrieved from http://www.inthelibrarywiththeleadpipe.org/2015/lis-diversity/

Hathcock, A. (2019). ALAMW: What happened, and what should happen next. Retrieved from https://aprilhathcock.wordpress.com/2019/01/30/alamw-what-happened-and-what-should-happen-next/

McKenzie, L. (2018). Harassment of MIT libraries director denounced. Retrieved from https://www.insidehighered.com/quicktakes/2018/03/13/harassment-mit-libraries-director-denou nced

McKenzie, L. (2019). Racism and the American Library Association. Retrieved from https://www.insidehighered.com/news/2019/02/01/american-library-association-criticized-response-racism-complaint

Swift, A. (2017). Americans' worries about race relations at record high. Retrieved from https://news.gallup.com/poll/206057/americans-worry-race-relations-record-high.aspx

Part I

Why Diversity and Inclusion Matter

Chapter One

From Whence We Come

A Historical Perspective

Janice M. Young and John L. Donovan

You may shoot me with your words, You may cut me with your eyes, You may kill me with your hatefulness, But still, like air, I'll rise.

—Maya Angelou

The achievements and contributions of African American pioneers in librarianship, who succeeded and excelled in their careers despite the many obstacles of racism, sexism, ageism, and so forth, blazed a path for women and librarians of color to self-actualize careers as librarians. Their dedication in starting discussions about implementing inclusion policies and programs brought about realist conversations regarding the perception of marginalized groups in homogeneous institutions. These trailblazing men and women, who affirmed their legitimacy as librarians during a time in American history that was governed under "separate but equal" legislation, confronted segregation, fought negative stigmatization, and sought equal treatment. By challenging unjust and discriminatory principles and policies and implementing institutional changes of cultural, organizational integrity and authentic leadership, they bequeathed to librarianship their movements, opportunities, and obstacles in building stronger, inclusive communities. Leveraging their achievements through hard-fought battles, these pioneers and trailblazers, too many to name and include in this chapter, left a legacy for the next generation of librarians that bridged the past to the present. From whence we come is a road paved with sacrifice, perseverance, courage, and strength, valuing diversity and inclusion in perpetuating *change* that leads to access, opportunities, and growth for women and librarians of color.

ON THIS ROCK SHALL I BUILD

Cultivating a Community

Community is a powerful motivating force, which often brings out the very best people have to offer (Pinchot & Pinchot, 1997, p. 14). When leaders place an emphasis on sharing an organization's vision, all members can participate in the shared vision of the institution. One such example is Reverend Thomas Fountain Blue, who delivered the opening address at a conference of Black librarians at Hampton Institute in 1927 entitled "Arousing Community Interest in the Library" (Smith, 1998, p. 85).

Reverend Thomas Fountain Blue (1866–1935)

Born to parents who were former slaves, Thomas Fountain Blue seemed predestined for a life of leadership and service. He attended Hampton Normal and Agricultural Institute from 1885 to 1888. In his commencement speech at Hampton, he spoke about devoting himself to helping improve circumstances for African Americans by cultivating a community of inclusion (Wright, 1955, p. 4). In 1905, Thomas Fountain Blue became the first African American to head a public library. His expectation on "high quality, community interest, varied services and professional responsibilities that he held himself to, was also expected of his staff" (Wright, 1955, p. 14). The Western Colored Branch was the first Carnegie colored library in Louisville, Kentucky, to offer service exclusively to African Americans (Jones, 2002, p. 52). The building is still standing at the corner of 10th and Chestnut Streets (Jones, 2002, p. 52). Although Blue had not received formal training in librarianship, his commitment of service and leadership acumen earned him the joint appointment of the Western Colored Branch Library and the newly constructed Eastern Colored Branch Library that opened its doors on January 28, 1914 (Wright, 1955, p. 18). Reverend Blue "developed a four-to-six-month apprentice training program for African-American librarians that combined education and practical work experience" (Whitmire, 2014, p. 9). The Western Colored Branch Library trained local and out-of-state students. The "library classes held at Western Branch represented the first library-training program for African-Americans in the United States" (Jones, 2002, p. 54).

Reverend Blue wanted trained library staff working in the Western Colored Branch Library. To do this, "courses were established, and staff received lectures on classification, cataloging, and general library information was given to the staff" (Wright, 1955, p. 17). In the early 20th century, the American South provided no library school for African Americans seeking a career in librarianship. Blue's vision of community, commitment, and dedication was shared not only with the librarians and the staff employed at the two Negro branch libraries in Louisville, Kentucky, but also with all who entered the Western Colored Branch Library and the Eastern Colored Branch Library. Librarianship benefited from Blue's dedication to lead a library that serviced the needs of Louisville's African American community and was a direct reflection of his contribution to history as an African American librarian. In 1922, he continued his role as trailblazer by being the first African American to deliver a speech before the American Library Association (ALA; Smith, 1998, p. 85).

BEING THE *FIRST*: ACCOLADES AND ACQUISITIONS

Women and Minorities

Institutional Culture of Change

The first half of the 20th century was marked by public libraries with limited access for African Americans due to segregated libraries throughout the South, a "region identified with White supremacy, poverty, and ignorance—and where public library development in general lagged behind that in the Northeast and Midwest" (Knott, 2016, p. 3). A great challenge for aspiring African American librarians was to find a school administration that would allow them to not only attend a traditionally White library school but also complete an advanced degree program in library science. However, even after having the opportunity to earn a degree, it was very difficult for African American librarians to obtain employment in their chosen profession due to institutionalized racism. According to Elonnie Junius (E. J.) Josey (1970), a pioneer educator and librarian, "Black librarians were unseen, unheard, and unknown," as White librarians in the United States "had ignored or did not consider them vital to the operation of libraries in America" (p. 82). Included in this chapter are the stories of four women who earned accolades as being "first" in many ways: Virginia Proctor Powell Florence, Eliza Atkins Gleason, Virginia Lacy Jones, and Clara Stanton Jones. These women are a great testament in overcoming discrimination and racism in the library profession and serving as role models of librarianship that expanded opportunities for African Americans in education, research, politics, and leadership (Biddle, 1993, p. 118).

Virginia Proctor Powell Florence (1903–1991)

In 1922, officials of the Carnegie Library School in Pittsburgh, Pennsylvania, were confronted with a dilemma. Virginia Proctor Powell Florence, a young African American woman who had successfully earned a degree in education from Oberlin College in Ohio, had applied for admission to the Carnegie

Library School. Carnegie school officials were concerned not only that White students at the school would react poorly and be embarrassed having a fellow student who was Black but also that the school would have a difficult time finding a library willing to hire an African American graduate (Gunn, 1989, pp. 155–157). Despite their reservations, Carnegie officials opted to let her enter the library sciences program. While completing her practical studies during her second semester at the school, Florence participated in a work experience program that required her to learn the duties of her occupation at library branches in the Pittsburgh area. It was in this setting that she would labor under occupational restrictions that included not being able to interact directly with White patrons and only being able to observe the White librarians carrying out their duties (especially when it came to interacting with children during the library storytelling hour). Even though Florence had to endure such limited practical skills training, she developed "a reputation as a fast learner who was well liked by all who came to know her." Following her graduation from Carnegie in 1923, she "became the first African American woman to complete a professional education program in librarianship" (Dawson, 2000, p. 57).

Following graduation, Florence worked at a Pittsburgh library before accepting an employment opportunity at the New York Public Library. After working at various branches within the New York Public Library system through 1927, she became the first African American to take and pass the librarian examination for New York high schools, which resulted in her appointment as the librarian for Brooklyn's Seward Park High School, a position she would hold until 1931. After taking a seven-year hiatus from work, she later served as the librarian for Cardozo High School in Washington, DC, followed by a librarian position at the Maggie L. Walker Senior High School in Richmond, Virginia, until her retirement in 1965 (Gunn, 1989, p. 156).

Although her graduation from the Carnegie Library School in 1923 was a milestone in librarianship, Florence contended in a 1980 interview that "she was an experiment and that the school did not want to send a signal that Blacks could feel free to apply for admission" (Gunn, 1989, p. 157). However, her admission to the library school opened a door that would later be entered by two African American women pursuing higher degrees in library science.

Organizational Integrity

Homogenous Culture

By the mid-1940s, the opportunity for African American women to obtain higher degrees in library science could be found at the University of Chicago.

This access to an advanced degree program was accompanied by an opportunity for scholarly research into the state of libraries in the United States, especially those in the South, and the challenges of obtaining African American access to public-use facilities. This time frame also led to more opportunities for African Americans to serve on committees and move into leadership positions within the ALA.

Dr. Eliza Atkins Gleason (1909–2009)

In 1940, Eliza Atkins Gleason was the first African American woman to obtain a PhD degree in library science, from the University of Chicago. Her dissertation, "The Government and Administration of Public Library Service to Negroes in the South," was published in 1941 as *The Southern Negro and the Public Library: A Study of the Government and Administration of Public Library Service to Negroes in the South* (Dawson, 2000; Ohles, Ohles, & Ramsay, 1997). Gleason's research examined the state of libraries in the South during the Jim Crow era, when public facilities, such as libraries, were required under the direction of the Supreme Court ruling of *Plessy v. Ferguson* to be substantially equal for both Blacks and Whites. She found that library-use facilities for African Americans were "inadequate and inferior to those for the general public," with 2 million African Americans in areas where there were "libraries for White persons but none for Negroes" (Kelley, 1942, p. 556). Gleason made the case in *The Southern Negro and the Public Library* that the historic and legal factors that led to Jim Crow segregation would take time to change, but eventually, communities would realize that it would be in their economic interests to focus on "providing one good public library for all races," instead of facing the "economic impossibility of building two first-rate public library systems—one for the Negro and one for the White group" (Gleason, 1941, p. 188). She also advocated that a library school for African Americans be opened to provide professional library services training. Her study was the "first comprehensive study of public library services for African-Americans" (Dawson, 2000, p. 57).

In line with the recommendation from her book, and shortly after completing her dissertation, in 1940 Gleason was selected as the first dean of the School of Library Service at Atlanta University (AU), a school founded to train African American librarians. While serving as dean of AU, Gleason was also the first African American to sit on the board of the ALA. Additionally, it was at AU that she worked with Virginia Lacy Jones, who was serving on the staff of the library school as a full-time faculty member.

Virginia Lacy Jones (1912–1984)

Virginia Lacy Jones encountered the segregationist policies of the South that Gleason examined in *The Southern Negro and the Public Library* while working on her bachelor of library science (BLS) degree at the Hampton Institute in Virginia (Josey, 1970). The Hampton Library School at Hampton Institute, established in 1925 as a library school for African Americans to earn a BLS degree, closed in June 1939 due to a lack of funding to continue the school (Smith, 1940). In 1935, Jones attended her first ALA conference, where she described that the presence of African American students "created great confusion at the meeting" (Josey, 1970, p. 26). After finding that she and her fellow students were seated in segregated sections of the conference and denied entry to exhibits at the hotel in which the meeting was held, complaints were made to ALA leadership that resulted in the organization adopting "a policy not to meet again in a city where all librarians could not attend the meeting without embarrassment" (Josey, 1970, p. 26). It was this experience at an ALA meeting in Richmond that led to changes in organizational policies regarding the treatment of African American librarians.

Starting in 1937, Jones enrolled in an advanced degree program in librarianship at the University of Illinois and was given a fellowship to pursue her studies under the stipulation that she would contribute "to library development for Negroes in the South" (Josey, 1970, p. 78). In 1941, she was hired as a founding faculty member of the School of Library Service at AU. She taught literature courses for children, library services for schools, and classifying and cataloging classes. Jones took a two-year hiatus from teaching in 1943 after she accepted another fellowship to pursue a PhD degree in library science at the University of Chicago. Upon completion of her dissertation, "The Problems of Negro Public High Schools in Selected Southern Cities," she became the second African American to earn a librarianship doctoral degree (Josey, 1970, p. 80).

In 1945, Jones accepted the position of dean of the School of Library Service at AU when Eliza Atkins Gleason stepped down. Under Jones's leadership, the school's curriculum was expanded, and students were eventually able to earn the BLS degree, as well as a master of library science degree (Ohles, Ohles, & Ramsay, 1997, p. 182). Over the next two decades, while serving as dean, Jones dedicated her efforts in librarianship to programs that would improve library services for African Americans throughout the country. In 1967, she became the first African American president of the American Association of Library Schools, now known as the Association for Library and Information and Science Education (Dawson, 2000, p. 58). From 1967 to 1970, Jones served on the president of the United States' Advisory Council on Library Research and Training Projects. Additionally, she was awarded the Melvil Dewey Award in 1973 and the Joseph W. Lippincott Award in 1977 for librarian excellence, becoming the first African American to receive either award from the ALA (Ohles, Ohles, & Ramsay, 1997, p. 183). She was recognized as "a giant in library education and was known as the 'dean of library school deans' because her career as dean (36 years) was longer than any of her contemporaries" (Josey, 1970, p. 82). In assessing the challenges faced by White and African American librarians, Jones stated, "Both groups will have to continue to work with open minds and honest efforts to evaluate each other not by color of skin and ethnic background but on the basis of true merit" (Josey, 1970, p. 41).

Perception Is Reality

Leading Change

The accomplishments of both Gleason and Jones expanded opportunities for African Americans in librarian education and leadership positions. According to Josey (1970), the challenges faced by Black librarians during the 20th century shaped them "personally and professionally" for leadership roles in "educational reform" and librarianship (p. xvi). The trailblazing work of Clara Stanton Jones encapsulated this quest for excellence in library science.

Clara Stanton Jones (1913–2012)

After working 24 years as a librarian in the Detroit Public Library (DPL) system, Clara Stanton Jones was appointed director of the DPL. She served from 1970 to 1978 and was both the first woman and the first African American to be selected for this leadership position. Jones was the third woman to lead a major public library in a U.S. city and the first African American to lead a major public library system in the United States (Butler, 1997; Wheeler, 2012). Due to her race, she faced negative comments for being selected for this position (two library board members quit), despite being eminently qualified from her experience working within the Detroit Public Library system. In reflecting on her accomplishments, Jones stated that she "remembered how our people, Black people, suffered for many generations in slavery, enduring far worse undeserved suffering" than she had and that she was "inspired by their wonderful example" (McCook, 1998, p. 44). She also added that she gave her best as director for nearly nine years and that she "loved every minute of it" (McCook, 1998, p. 44).

In 1976, Jones achieved another major milestone when she was elected as the first African American president of the ALA. Jones contended that the "civil rights movement of the '50s and '60s helped greatly to democratize ALA along with other professional organizations" (McCook, 1998, p. 51) and allowed her to combat racism within the library profession. When asked to describe her experience in dealing with issues related to race in her rise as director of the Detroit Public Library system and president of the ALA, Jones responded,

People said, "How did you go through that business of being so battered over your appointment and other things with regard to race?" The thing I do is to remember my foreparents, my forebearers, all of the Black people who went through generations of slavery and the years after slavery that were not very different from slavery. People lived without the conveniences and privilege that I had. The courage that they showed: how could I cry over not being welcomed to a great opportunity? I just can't. I have to try to emulate those men and women, and that's my star that I follow. That's [the] source of my inspiration. That's the source of my pride as a human being. (McCook, 1998, p. 56)

The trailblazing experiences of Virginia Proctor Powell Florence, Eliza Atkins Gleason, Virginia Lacy Jones, and Clara Stanton Jones are inspirational accounts reflecting the pioneering efforts of African American women in the field of librarianship who served as role models in the fields of education, research, and leadership studies.

FROM CONFLICT TO COLLABORATION

Authentic Leadership

Authentic leadership and integrity are placed in the broader scope of positive organizational behavior or positive organizational scholarship. It is the collective bargaining impetus that "a single individual as long as he or she is acting on behalf of a group as a representative of the group and the direct actions is to improve the condition of the group" (Wright & Taylor, 1998, p. 649). Integrity is not a matter of words alone; it requires *acting* in accordance with rational principles and values (Becker, 1998, p. 157). Organizations based on integrity model their values and systematically cultivate a culture of trust and respect. It is a breach of integrity to know that one is right but then proceeds to defy the right in practice. It is not a breach of integrity but a moral obligation to change one's views if one finds that some idea one holds is wrong (Becker, 1998, p. 157).

Dr. Elonnie Junius Josey (1924–2009)

E. J. Josey was the first African American male elected president of the ALA and the "first black librarian to be accepted as a member of the Georgia Library Association" (Smith, 1998, pp. 670–671). He graduated from Howard University in 1949, completed a master's degree from Columbia University in 1950, and graduated with a library science degree from the New York State College for Teachers in Albany, New York, in 1953 (Josey, 1962, p. 492). At an ALA conference in 1964, Josey authored a resolution forbidding ALA officers and staff from participating in state associations that denied membership to Black librarians (Smith, 1998, p. 671). It was at the 1970 ALA Annual Conference in Detroit that Josey established the Black Caucus of the ALA (BCALA; Josey, 1970, p. 346). The purpose of the Black Caucus "was to address the many issues facing the nation and the hesitancy of the library profession to respond to the problems of institutional racism, poverty, the lack of educational, employment and promotional opportunities for black and other minorities" (Smith, 1998, p. 671). As a leader, scholar, teacher, mentor, and activist, Josey campaigned tirelessly to recruit African American students into the master and doctoral programs in library and information science in an effort to "fight the indignities, the patronizing attitudes, the insults and small humiliations borne by most black people" (Josey, 1970, p. 347).

Josey authored many articles and several books that addressed the plight of African American librarians, including but not limited to *The Handbook of Black Librarianship*, *What Black Librarians Are Saying*, and *Opportunities for Minorities in Librarianship* (Josey, 1970, p. 351). During his four decades as a member of the oldest and largest library association in the world, Josey chaired many committees, was elected to council in 1970, and began a term on the executive board in 1979 (Smith, 1998, p. 671). Josey authored and coauthored groundbreaking resolutions "to right things that are wrong" (Josey, 1970, p. 349). He and Clara Jackson served as coauthors of the resolution to establish the Standing Committee on the Status of Women in Librarianship. It was in the 1970s that Josey (1970) said,

> I began the real fight for librarians and libraries, and Black people in South Africa.
> Whenever I saw a void in leadership, I took the opportunity to try to encourage my colleagues to "right things that are wrong." I did not run from the task even though I might have been engaged in many other activities at the time. Whenever I saw injustice, I tried to right it. (p. 349)

When Josey passed away in Washington, North Carolina, on July 3, 2009, our profession suffered a devastating loss of a librarian, scholar, activist, teacher, and friend. Josey bequeathed "45 years of his life devoted to active service to the library profession" (Smith, 1998, p. 670) and was particularly noted for his efforts on behalf of libraries and librarians suffering under the oppression of racism, sexism, ageism, and so forth. He looked into the future and shared his vision, values, and goals to cultivate a community of inclusion. Even today "libraries of all types are undergoing a hectic period reexamining goals and cherished beliefs" (McPheeters & Dalton, 1988, p. 107).

Equality and Access

The core task of a leader is to create the condition for civic or institutional engagement. They do this through the power they have to name the debate and design gatherings (Block, 2009, p. 86).

Diversity and Inclusion

Morality alone doesn't change organizational culture or an institution's priorities. Instituting change, not for the sake of change alone, but for a change that is the catalyst for creating fairness when and where it doesn't exist, requires moving organizations from separate points of view to inclusiveness and migrating people from conflict to collaboration that allows for all to contribute at the highest possible level (Childs, 2005, p. 73).

Dr. Joseph Harry Reason (1905–1997)

Dr. Joseph Reason, director of libraries at Howard University, was the first African American to serve as president of the Association of College and Research Libraries (ACRL). In 1928, he graduated summa cum laude with a bachelor of arts degree in history from New Orleans University (Davis, 2003, p. 182). Reason later went on to earn his PhD in romance languages, having been awarded a "$250 scholarship to aid the completion of doctoral studies at the Catholic University of America from the Omega Psi Phi fraternity" (Aldridge, 1981, p. 35).

Reason majored in library science as a student at Columbia University's School of Library Service and graduated from the school in 1936 (Davis, 2003, p. 182). It was at the 1938 Florida Library Association annual convention in St. Petersburg that he presented his paper titled "Library Services for Negroes in Florida" (Davis, 2003, p. 184). From 1938 to 1946, he was a reference librarian at Howard University and become director of libraries at Howard in 1946, a position he retained for 25 years (Caris, 2015). Reason's dedication to service for students and faculty members at Howard University were evident in his beliefs that "the library existed to provide greater stimulation to the cultural needs of the student beyond the confines of the regular curriculum, that the library helps in developing students' attitudes toward continuing their education after graduation, and that the library can foster the idea of education as a continuing process" (Davis, 2003, p. 184).

In 1965, Reason was nominated for ALA president, which was historically significant because he was the first Black to be nominated. Robert Pearson wrote in an article that Reason had an air of "quiet strength of trying to prove nothing; a suggestion of a vast reserve of sense and drive; a suggestion which may be due in part to height; in part to impeccable tone production, and in part a total lack of 'fidgets,' but which one would like to suppose has its principle source in character and intellect" (as cited in Davis, 2003, p. 185).

Active in both the ALA and ACRL, Reason authored several articles that were published in the *Negro College Quarterly*, articles that offered "opportunities for all persons interested in education a chance to share their research findings on the racial climate of universities and colleges during that time" (Davis, 2003, p. 184). His collaboration with Virginia Lacy Jones produced the column "College Notes and News" (p. 184).

A keystone moment in Reason's career was his memorable address at the first Tennessee Governor's Conference held on November 3, 1967, in the War Memorial Auditorium in Nashville, Tennessee (Davis, 2003, p. 186). Reason stated that he felt automation and cooperation were interrelated and was not worried about what would happen to libraries as a result of automatic systems. "Automation is far more likely to upgrade the profession of librarianship than to replace it" (Davis, 2003, p. 186).

WHO WILL WRITE OUR LEGACY?

Our librarian ancestors took their fight to the doorsteps of the ALA to try to right a wrong for women and librarians of color. To do what is right is noble, but it is not always the catalyst in desiring to ensure that everyone has the same level of equality, access, retention, and advancement. Despite an organizational commitment to the advancement of diversity initiatives, women and people of color continue to be underrepresented in master of library and information science (MLIS) graduate programs, leadership positions, and senior management posts in librarianship. Marginalized groups recognize discriminatory practices in the workplace despite how well they are camouflaged. When witnessing the lack of marginalized individuals' representation in management positions that determine hiring and promotion decisions, what is evident is not an inclusive and diverse culture. There is an absence of women and minorities assigned to work on high-profile projects in many organizations, and they often encounter passive-aggressive tactics used to attack their credibility, reputation, and competency.

The librarians included in this chapter and others not mentioned paved the way for members of marginalized groups with careers in librarianship. They challenged their organizations, institutions, and leadership to give way to "equality of opportunity" (Josey, 1970, p. 354) by resolving conflict through collaboration and staying vigilant when sexism, racism, ageism, and so forth jeopardized hard-won inroads. And so, it is with these tools and perspectives that librarianship in the 21st century must explore our legacy from whence we come.

REFERENCES

Aldridge, M. L. (Ed.). (1981). *Opportunity: Journal of Negro life* (Vol. 25). New York: Department of Research and Investigations, National Urban League.

Becker, T. E. (1998). Integrity in organizations: Beyond honesty and conscientiousness. *Academy of Management Review, 23*(1), 154–161. Retrieved from https://doi.org/10.5465/amr.1998.192969

Biddle, S. F. (1993). *Culture keepers: Enlightening and empowering our communities; souvenir program*. Newark, NJ: Black Caucus of the American Library Association.

Block, P. (2009). *Community: The structure of belonging*. San Francisco: Berrett-Koehler.

Butler, M. E. (1997). *Black women stirring the waters*. Oakland, CA: Marcus Books. Retrieved from http://books.google.com/books?id=_Od2AAAAMAAJ

Caris, E. (2015, March 11). Meet the ACRL presidents: Joseph Henry Reason | ACRL 75th anniversary website. Retrieved October 18, 2018, from ttps://acrl.ala.org/acrl75/?p=854

Childs, T. J. J. (2005). Managing workforce diversity at IBM: A global HR topic that has arrived. *Human Resource Management, 44*(1), 73–77. Retrieved from https://doi.org/10.1002/hrm.20042

Davis, D. (2003). *Dictionary of American library biography: Second supplement*. Westport, CT: Libraries Unlimited.

Dawson, A. (2000). Celebrating African American librarians and librarianship. *Library Trends, 49*(1), 49–87.

Gleason, Eliza V. A. (1941). *The southern Negro and the public library: A study of the government and administration of public library service to Negroes in the South*. Chicago: University of Chicago Press.

Gunn, A. C. (1989). A Black woman wants to be a professional. *American Libraries, 20*, 154–157.

Jones, R. F. (2002). *Library service to African Americans in Kentucky, from the Reconstruction era to the 1960s*. Jefferson, NC: McFarland.

Josey, E. J. (1962). The role of the college library staff in instruction in the use of the library. *College of Research Libraries, 23*(6), 492–498.

Josey, E. J. (1970). *The Black librarian in America*. Metuchen, NJ: Scarecrow Press.

Kelley, D. M. (1942). Review of *Review of the southern Negro and the public library: A study of the government and administration of public library service to Negroes in the South*, by E. A. Gleason. *Elementary School Journal, 42*(7), 555–556.

Knott, C. (2016). *Not free, not for all*. Amherst: University of Massachusetts Press.

McCook, K. de la P. (1998). *Women of color in librarianship: An oral history*. Chicago, IL: American Library Association.

McPheeters, A. L., & Dalton, J. (1988). *Library service in black and white: Some personal recollections, 1921–1980*. Metuchen, NJ: Scarecrow Press.

Ohles, F., Ohles, S. M., & Ramsay, J. G. (1997). *Biographical dictionary of modern American educators*. Westport, CT: Greenwood Press.

Pinchot, G., & Pinchot, E. (1997). Organizations that encourage integrity. *Journal for Quality and Participation; Cincinnati, 20*(2), 10–19.

Smith, J. C. (1998). *Notable Black American men*. Detroit: Gale Research.

Smith, S. L. (1940). The passing of the Hampton Library School. *Journal of Negro Education, 9*(1), 51–58. Retrieved http://dx.doi.org/10.2307/2292881

Wheeler, M. (2012). Remembering Clara Stanton Jones. *Library Journal*. Retrieved from https://lj.libraryjournal.com/2012/12/opinion/backtalk/remembering-clara-stanton-jones-backtalk/

Whitmire, E. (2014). *Regina Anderson Andrews, Harlem renaissance librarian*. Chicago: University of Illinois Press.

Wright, L. T. (1955). *Thomas Fountain Blue, pioneer librarian, 1866–1935*. Atlanta: Atlanta University. Retrieved from ETD Collection for AUC Robert W. Woodruff Library.

Wright, S. C., & Taylor, D. M. (1998). Responding to tokenism: Individual action in the face of collective injustice. *European Journal of Social Psychology, 28*(4), 647–667.

Chapter Two

Overview of Diversity and Inclusion Literature and Research

1970–2017

Xan Y. Goodman

Why should the world be over-wise. In counting all our tears and signs? Nay, let them only see us, while We wear the mask.

—Paul Laurence Dunbar

BACKGROUND: DIVERSITY AND INCLUSION RESEARCH AND ITS IMPORTANCE TO LIBRARIES

Diversity and inclusion research in the field of librarianship has been a winding road of inquiry. In 1876, only one year before the end of the Reconstruction period in the United States, the official organization of librarians, the American Library Association (ALA), was formed by Melvil Dewey in Philadelphia (Ollé, 1977). Only a mere 14 years earlier, legalized slavery had ended in the United States (Lauren, 1996). The context of library staff and library facilities operating in the United States has been within the social milieu in which they are planted. Libraries and librarians exist in society and respond to social norms and values, as well as the times in which libraries exist and in which librarians practice their profession. Such is the ground from which this chapter explores diversity and inclusion literature and research in librarianship for the United States from 1970 to 2017.

Discourses about diversity and librarianship in the United States have been necessarily linked to race, and this is needful in light of the founding of the country. When the United States was birthed, many of the founding fathers were or had been slaveowners at some point in time. Native peoples were also subject to slaughter. Principles enshrined in the founding documents stated "all men are created equal," yet the dissonance of owning human beings and the lack of equal treatment granted to enslaved African peoples escaped the founding fathers, steeping them in contradiction, hypocrisy, and conflict. It is in this soil soaked in the rhetoric of freedom, exceptionalism, and equality that American libraries were founded. Removing, ignoring, or making an attempt to erase race from discussions related to libraries would ignore the roots of race as a founding principle that shaped America and its library services from the start.

It is with this lens that diversity and inclusion research is approached in this chapter with the acknowledgment that race in the United States is foundational. Capers (2007) says, "Black, after all, is still the figure in which power relationships of master/slave, civilized/primitive, enlightened/backward, good/evil have been embodied in the American subconscious" (p. 4). Library research presented in this text is limited to those articles that ask a diversity or inclusion question and seek to answer that question using either qualitative or quantitative research methods. An attempt is also made to provide historical context for library diversity and inclusion research by linking it to U.S. societal norms. Additionally, a discussion of changing definitions of *diversity* and *inclusion research literature* from this period is included.

This chapter does not cover research about critical librarianship, as there are excellent resources available on this topic (see "Additional Reading" at the end of this chapter). A broad range of proposed frameworks, published essays, and books that are diversity related are also excluded. Treatment of the research presented is not done using the methodology of a systematic review; therefore, not all research literature is included, limiting the scope of this chapter coverage.

DIVERSITY, 1970–1980

At the start of the 1970s, there were cries to establish ethnic studies programs as part of the cultural landscape and in light of turbulent times throughout the United States that began in the 1960s: the Stonewall movement, the slaying of Dr. King, turmoil with the American Indian movement, and the Black Panther movement (Jones, 1999). However, when searching the two premier library literature databases (Library and Information Sciences Abstracts and Library Literature and Information Science) for research grounded in quantitative or qualitative methods, only 15 articles were located, and none were research based. Research in library and information science in the 1970s and 1980s was not yet in the form of research later seen in the profession. The limitations of using the search terms *diversity*, *research*, and *libraries* and the parameters of quantitative or qualitative research may have resulted in the small number of articles retrieved.

In a review of the articles retrieved, there is a mention of diversity as it relates to equal access in a paper by Becker (1978) presented to the Institute on Federal Documents and Information Accessibility, where he referred to the decade 1967–1977 as the Information Decade. Becker described the diverse information landscape of the decade and outlined ways in which information policy and its relevance to various stakeholders might be viewed. He noted the passage of the 1974 Privacy Act as a response to concerns related to privacy and computerized data storage. At the end of his paper, Becker outlined a set of principles for information policy relevant to this research in which he stated, "We are dedicated to the widest possible utilization of this equal resource and the right of all people to have equal opportunity of access to it according to their individual needs" (Becker, 1978, p. 14).

To gain more insight into diversity themes, the ALA and developments in that organization were explored. Ethnic caucuses were established within the ALA from 1970 to 1980; however, uncovering the historical research about the formation of these caucuses was difficult to locate in the indexed scholarly databases. Tze-Chung Li (1979) wrote a profile of Chinese American librarians and noted the annual conference of Chinese librarians held in Detroit, Michigan, and the contributions of Chinese American librarians as a theme for that conference.

A champion of diversity whose work also did not appear in the literature search was Dr. Elonnie J. Josey, who wrote extensive essays and commentary about issues related to race, segregation, and librarianship (Abdullahi & Josey, 2002; Jackson, Herling, & Josey, 1976; Josey, 1971; 1972). Josey founded the Black Caucus of the American Library Association (BCALA) in 1970. Other ethnic caucuses followed: REFORMA, the National Association to Promote Library and Information Services to Latinos and the Spanish Speaking, 1971; the Asian American Library Caucus, 1975; and the American Indian Library Association (AILA), 1978 (Echavarria & Wertheimer, 1997). The Asian Pacific American Library Association (APALA) was founded in 1980 (Yamashita, 2000). Diversity in librarianship during this decade focused on the pressing issues relevant to the times, building a place within the profession for the voices of diverse librarians in the form of ethnic caucuses. Though librarians published books and essays during this decade, the range of research articles is limited.

Definitions

Definitions surrounding the language of diversity research are important and are often time-bound. For example, to speak of diversity in the decade between 1970 and 1980 is dissimilar from discussions of diversity in the years between 2010 and 2017. Language morphs and twists to convey different meanings, and such is the case with diversity research and libraries. From 1970 through the late 1990s, discussions around diversity were framed with the words *diversity, cultural diversity, affirmative action*, and *multicultural-ism. Diversity* was a burgeoning term in the 1970s that was largely focused on ethnicity and race, thus the formation of ALA ethnic caucuses and affinity groups. Affirmative action was and might still be a hot-button term, as it describes legal remedies to rectify a harm and an active effort to improve employment or educational opportunities for members of minority groups and for women. Affirmative action "consisted of policies, programs, and procedures that give preferences to minorities and women in job hiring, admission to institutions of higher education, the awarding of government contracts, and other social benefits. The typical criteria for affirmative action are race, disability, gender, ethnic origin, and age" (Affirmative Action, 2018).

DIVERSITY, MULTICULTURALISM, AND INCLUSION, 1980–1990

Attitudes toward cultural diversity shifted in the 1980s as government-spon-sored remedies to address affirmative action were attacked. In the 1980s and early 1990s, the stew pot of diversity began to shift to cultural diversity and multiculturalism. Abdullahi and Josey (2002) described cultural diversity as "equal participation of men and women in organizations regardless of race, ethnicity, or gender. It also includes persons who are physically challenged as well as those who are concerned about sexual orientation" (p. 11). There was a degree of intersectionality represented in the term *cultural diversity*, which acknowledged changes in U.S. law with passage of the Americans With Disabilities Act (1990).

Du Mont, Buttlar, and Caynon (1994) made the case for *multiculturalism*, a popular term in the 1990s, in their compendium of essays *Multiculturalism in Libraries*. Through the frame of cultural diversity and pluralism, these essays offered a historical melting-pot approach to diversity that looked backward and forward to present solutions of how libraries approached themes of diversity. In response to teacher training, researchers described the need for teachers to develop skill sets to engage with multicultural popula-tions (Abilock, 2006; Banks, 1997; Cruz-Jansen & Taylor, 2004; Gallavan, 2005). These authors encouraged an approach to multiculturalism that moved beyond recognition inherent in heroes and holidays, activities designed to integrate multicultural themes.

Inclusion or *inclusive* came into the lexicon of library research in the 1990s, though the term has been seen more frequently in the past 27 years. Searches in two primary library and information sciences databases for

1990–1999 found articles related to the terms. The American Association of Colleges and Universities (AAC&U) defines *inclusion* as

> active, intentional, and ongoing engagement with diversity—in the curriculum, in the co-curriculum, and in communities (intellectual, social, cultural, geographical) with which individuals might connect—in ways that increase awareness, content knowledge, cognitive sophistication, and empathic understanding of the complex ways individuals interact within systems and institutions. (AAC&U, 2013)

DIVERSITY, MULTICULTURALISM, AND INCLUSION, 1990–2000

In 1989 the United States was emerging from a long-standing Cold War with Russia (U.S.S.R.), and the Berlin Wall in East Berlin had opened amid surprise and delight. Libraries were growing and responding to new regulations to add accommodations prescribed in the newly passed Americans With Disabilities Act. Economic times were flush during the 1990s with the expansion of a new technology, the World Wide Web, which would change the way librarians work and how patrons access library collections and use library services.

Buttlar and Wynar (1993) conducted a study to examine the habits of authors who wrote about cultural pluralism and diversity for five major ethnic studies journals. They asked two research questions: How do these authors discover information? And how do they retrieve information for their use? The Buttlar and Wynar study is an example of a specific patron group—researchers—that examines cultural diversity and engages with diverse library collections. Greenfield, Rawan, and O'Neill (1993) described creating guides to support diverse viewpoints. In this narrative, four graduate students were hired to collaborate with librarians to develop eight guides for undergraduate library instruction and outreach, seven of which focused on nonmajority populations in higher education, including Native Americans and African Americans. The graduate students were trained in research methods, topic selection, and subject classification. Each guide included a personal statement from the student-author of the guide, and the project included a follow-up survey of the graduate students' thoughts about the process. Using a survey, Tjoumas (1993) examined acquisitions of American Indian literature for young people in public libraries. As a result of her research, she proposed the following recommendations: improve awareness of selection tools for Native American literature, such as specialized bibliography tools, increase funding to acquire resources, and examine goals and criteria for selection of collections related to Native American literature for children in public libraries.

DIVERSITY, MULTICULTURALISM, AND INCLUSION, 2000–2017

Jaeger, Bertot, and Franklin (2010) pointed out that there are issues beyond ethnicity in the discourse about inclusion within libraries: sexual orientation, disabilities, socioeconomic status (SES), and geographic disadvantage, including low levels of diversity among library and information science (LIS) faculty. Preparedness of post-trained librarians to effectively engage with diverse communities was another area of research. Mestre in her 2010 study presented research about librarians in academic and research libraries and how prepared they felt to work with diverse cultures. Her study outlined some of the on-the-job challenges librarians faced when working with diverse populations. Librarians felt they needed training when working with diverse groups (ethnic, racial, religious, and linguistic) on how to communicate, build coalitions, learn cultural nuances, and be approachable (Mestre, 2010). Mestre noted that librarians felt library school did not train them to work with multiple cultures, revealing that "less than one quarter of respondents to her survey said library school trained them to work with multiple cultures" (Mestre, 2010, p. 484). More than 60% of Mestre's survey respondents who were in multicultural positions did not intend to seek those types of positions, so they might not have sought out courses with multicultural or diversity tracks while in library school training (Mestre, 2010).

Damasco and Hodges's (2012) survey of academic librarians of color included those who self-identified as part of historically underrepresented groups. The survey questions focused on retention, promotion and tenure, and obstacles to promotion and tenure for librarians of color and offered free text entries to gather qualitative comments from librarians. Within library science there has not been much research about librarians of color and promotion and tenure. There is more research about faculty of color experiences in the academy, and Damasco and Hodges (2012) covered some of this literature in their article. Results of their research indicated that information mentoring was an "effective form of professional development" (p. 293), and organizations could better serve librarians of color by filling in gaps for supervisors when there was turnover. An example offered was disparate advice given to some colleagues while faculty of color floundered with unclear expectations: "While I am in a tenure-track position, I often feel that advice is definitely different depending on [senior] faculty perception of how much 'help' is needed" (Damasco & Hodges, 2012, p. 296). Damasco and Hodges concluded that effective strategies to help librarians of color could include increasing access to informal and formal networks, acknowledging minority burden of additional workloads, allowing for expectations that are not similar across the board, and exposing hidden racism in higher education.

Alabi's (2015) study on racial microaggressions in academic libraries, which was published toward the end of the presidency of Barack Obama, gave voice to what Damasco and Hodges (2012) described as hidden racism. This context is important because, at the start of President Obama's term, there was exuberance about a postracial America. In fact, discourses to that effect were prevalent in academic scholarly circles. As defined in the psychology literature, Alabi provided examples of microaggressions, micro-insults, and microinvalidations, distinguishing such overt acts as lynching to more subtle behaviors and actions. Her literature review discussed the toll that microaggressive behaviors have on students and faculty of color as they navigate environments where they experience these behaviors. In particular, Alabi noted that repeated exposure can "have negative consequences for promotion and tenure for faculty" (Alabi, 2015, p. 48).

Alabi's study is one of the only ones published in library literature that examined microaggressions with a research instrument. One hundred eighty-nine non-White and nonminority librarians responded to her survey, which was sent to three Association of College and Research Libraries (ACRL) LISTSERVs and posed two research questions: (1) Are academic librarians of color experiencing racial microaggressions from their library colleagues? and (2) Do White academic librarians observe these derogatory exchanges directed at minority colleagues? Respondents were asked to report their experiences with 20 microaggressions or to respond to observing colleagues who were recipients of microaggressive behavior. The differences between scores for minority librarians versus nonminority librarians were statistically significant. Minority librarians reported experiencing microaggressions at greater rates than nonminority librarians reported observing microaggressive activities. Limitations of the survey were noted, such as a lack of a controlled environment to verify microaggressive activity. The main conclusion was that librarians need to discuss racism to improve retention and recruitment of non-White librarians. In November 2016, Donald J. Trump was elected the 45th president of the United States. Globally, responses to his election varied. By the summer of 2017, a strong White nationalist movement was present in the United States, resulting in the August 12, 2017, death of Heather Heyer at a White nationalist march in Charlottesville, Virginia. On August 30, 2017, the Ithaka S+R released a report commissioned by the Andrew W. Mellon Foundation (Schonfeld & Sweeney, 2017). The report examined the demographics of Association of Research Libraries (ARL) libraries by race/ethnicity and gender and created a baseline for future researchers to examine issues of diversity, equity, and inclusion in ARL libraries. Also included in the data was employment type (exempt or nonexempt) and management level by category: nonexempt; nonsupervisory, exempt; midmanagement, exempt; and senior.

LIBRARY RESEARCH THEMES

The themes of library research in this chapter have addressed a wide range of topics, including

- studies that examined how to increase diverse faculty in library and information science programs;
- studies that improved the recruitment of diverse populations into the profession;
- research that explored the experiences of diverse librarians; and
- patron-service-related studies examining library response to diverse communities in collections, programs, and other areas.

CONCLUSION

Within librarianship, there is a lot of focus on the role of librarians working with diverse cultures. In other words, there is a tendency in the literature to focus on the patrons, faculties, staffs, or others whom librarians support and serve. What is missing is a strong research focus on how librarians perform within the often-small ecosystems in which they work, as well as the challenges that librarians of color experience working in dominant environments. There are elements for inclusive practices in libraries that extend to services, programs, physical spaces, hiring practices, and collections, and these are areas for further exploration (Elturk, 2003). The journey for research on diversity, multiculturalism, and inclusion continues.

REFERENCES

Abdullahi, I., & Josey, E. J. (2002). Why diversity in American libraries. *Library Management, 23*(1/2), 10–16. Retrieved from https://doi.org/10.1108/01435120210413544

Abilock, D. (2006). Educating students for cross-cultural proficiency. *Knowledge Quest; Chicago, 35*(2), 10–13.

Affirmative Action. (2018). In *Encyclopaedia Britannica* (Online). Britannica.com. Retrieved from https://www.britannica.com/topic/affirmative-action

Alabi, J. (2015). Racial microaggressions in academic libraries: Results of a survey of minority and non-minority librarians. *Journal of Academic Librarianship, 41*(1), 47–53. Retrieved from https://doi.org/10.1016/j.acalib.2014.10.008

American Association of Colleges and Universities (AAC&U). (2013, October 17). Making excellence inclusive. Retrieved from https://www.aacu.org/making-excellence-inclusive

Banks, J. A. (1997). *Educating citizens in a multicultural society.* New York: Teachers College Press.

Becker, J. (1978). The information decade. Presented at the Institute on Federal Documents and Information Accessibility, Washington, DC.

Buttlar, L., & Wynar, L. R. (1993). Cultural pluralism and ethnic diversity. *Collection Management, 16*(3), 13–33. Retrieved from https://doi.org/10.1300/J105v16n03_02

Capers, I. B. (2007). *Reading back, reading Black* (SSRN Scholarly Paper No. ID 960496). Rochester, NY: Social Science Research Network. Retrieved from https://papers.ssrn.com/abstract=960496

Cruz-Jansen, M. I., & Taylor, M. (2004). Hitting the ground running: Why introductory teacher education courses should deal with multiculturalism. *Multicultural Education, 12*(1), 16–23.

Damasco, I. T., & Hodges, D. (2012). Tenure and promotion experiences of academic librarians of color. *College and Research Libraries, 73*(3), 279–301. Retrieved from https://doi.org/10.5860/crl-244

Du Mont, R. R., Buttlar, L., & Caynon, W. A. (1994). *Multiculturalism in libraries*. Westport, CT: Greenwood Press.

Echavarria, T., & Wertheimer, A. B. (1997). Surveying the role of ethnic-American library associations. *Library Trends, 46*(2), 373–391.

Elturk, G. (2003). Diversity and cultural competency. *Colorado Libraries, 29*(4), 5–7.

Gallavan, N. P. (2005). Helping teachers unpack their "invisible knapsacks." *Multicultural Education, 13*(1), 36.

Greenfield, L., Rawan, A., & O'Neill, C. (1993). The diversity research guide program. *Acquisitions Librarian, 5*(9–10), 115–129. Retrieved from https://doi.org/10.1300/J101v05n09_12

Jackson, S. L., Herling, E. B., & Josey, E. J. (1976). *A century of service: Librarianship in the United States and Canada*. Chicago: American Library Association.

Jaeger, P. T., Bertot, J. C., & Franklin, R. E. (2010). Diversity, inclusion, and underrepresented populations in LIS research. *Library Quarterly, 80*(2), 175–181. Retrieved from https://doi.org/10.1086/651053

Jones, P. A. (1999). *Libraries, immigrants, and the American experience*. Westport, CT: Greenwood Press.

Josey, E. J. (1971). Coddling segregation: The case for ALA action. *Library Journal, 96*(10), 1778–1779.

Josey, E. J. (1972). *What Black librarians are saying*. Metuchen, NJ: Scarecrow Press.

Lauren, P. G. (1996). *Power and prejudice: The politics and diplomacy of racial discrimination* (2nd ed.). Boulder: Westview Press.

Li, T.-C. (1979). Chinese contributions to American librarianship: A profile of Chinese-American librarians. *Journal of Library and Information Science; Taipei, 5*(1). Retrieved from http://search.proquest.com/docview/2001101313/citation/A931F0B5A8194E28PQ/1

Mestre, L. S. (2010). Librarians working with diverse populations: What impact does cultural competency training have on their efforts? *Journal of Academic Librarianship, 36*(6), 479–488. Retrieved from https://doi.org/10.1016/j.acalib.2010.08.003

Ollé, J. G. (1977). The Library Association and the American Library Association: Their first fifty years. *Journal of Librarianship, 9*(4), 247–260. Retrieved from https://doi.org/10.1177/096100067700900401

Schonfeld, R., & Sweeney, L. (2017). Inclusion, diversity, and equity: Members of the Association of Research Libraries; Employee demographics and director perspectives. *Ithaka S+R*. Retrieved from https://doi.org/10.18665/sr.304524

Tjoumas, R. (1993). Native American literature for young people: A survey of collection development methods in public libraries. *Library Trends, 41*(3), 493–523.

Yamashita, K. A. (2000). Asian/Pacific American Librarians Association: A history of APALA and its founders. *Library Trends, 49*(1), 88–109.

ADDITIONAL READING

Accardi, M., Drabinski, E., & Kumbier, A. (2014). *Critical library instruction*. Duluth, MN: Library Juice Press.

Tewell, E. (2015). A decade of critical information literacy: A review of the literature. *Comminfolit, 9*(1), 24–43. doi:10.15760/comminfolit.2015.9.1.174

Tewell, E. (2018). The practice and promise of critical information literacy: Academic librarians' involvement in critical library instruction. *College and Research Libraries, 79*(1), 10. doi:10.5860/crl.79.1.10

Chapter Three

The Changing Face of Librarianship

Carenado Davis and Tristan Ebron

Diversity is not a box to check, but is a reality that should be deeply felt, held, and valued by all of us. Diversity is not about one, two, or three in the room, but true diversity is half the room.

—Ava DuVernay

In the higher education environment, the lack of racial and ethnic diversity among college and university faculty is glaring, especially in regard to recruiting and retaining faculty of color. The same is true in librarianship. Despite the many claims by academic libraries that diversity is increasing in the profession, minority representation has changed very little in nearly two decades. Race and ethnicity are not the only issues of diversity and inclusion where individuals have had their needs ignored or marginalized, but the lack of racial and ethnic diversity remains too uncomfortably salient as it did nearly two decades ago (Visconti, 2015). According to Kelley (2013), African Americans and Hispanics are some of the strongest supporters of libraries, yet those in these demographics are some of the least represented among professional librarians. Kelley (2013) found that African Americans and Hispanics are much more likely to use library resources on a consistent basis, including accessing the Internet, using library computers, using meeting spaces, downloading e-books, and attending library events. African American and Hispanic support of libraries and their resources does not seem to translate into significant representation of African American and Hispanic librarians.

According to the American Library Association's (ALA) 2012 update to its *Diversity Counts* study, there were 118,666 credentialed librarians, and of that number, 6,160 were African American and 3,661 were Hispanic. Unfortunately, the study indicated the most disparaged group of librarians was

African American males, who according to Kelley (2013) included only 563 credentialed librarians, or 0.5% of the total librarian population. Academic libraries seem to have put very little effort into the effective recruitment and retention of minorities for librarian positions (Boisse & Dowell, 1987; Hathcock, 2015; Visconti, 2015). For the purposes of this chapter, we discuss why diversity in librarianship is important, whether diversity in librarianship is really changing, how to bridge the gaps, and the way to effectively change the face of librarianship to be more diverse and inclusive for minority librarians.

DIVERSITY MATTERS IN LIBRARIANSHIP

Abdullahi and Josey (2002) define *diversity* as the equal participation of men and women in an organization regardless of their gender, race, ethnicity, physical ability, or sexual orientation. For many years, a void has existed where certain populations of minorities have been neglected or ignored or not had their needs addressed, especially in regard to race and ethnicity and its impact on professional life. Abdullahi and Josey (2002) postulate that the diversity void in many libraries exists due to some members of the White majority believing that racism and discrimination are no longer issues in the workplace. It is important for diversity to be visible in libraries. Continued vigilance, work, and attention to visible diversity needs to continue so that libraries have adequate representation of the changing demographics and communities that are served (Hudson-Ward, 2014).

Diversity is still a challenge for libraries across the field. In 2009, only 11% of librarians in the United States were minorities. The *Diversity Counts* study shows that, of the 44,000 ALA members, only 12.9% are minorities. The most glaring statistic from the study reveals that 87.1% of librarians are White and 26% are between the ages of 55 and 64 (Hudson-Ward, 2014). Diversity is much more than a novel idea or talking points for presentations. It encompasses the whole person and includes age, culture, education, personality, skills, life experiences, sexual orientation, physical challenges, and gender, as well as race and ethnicity (Hudson-Ward, 2014). It is important to further the process of diversity by expelling stereotypes about librarians and the profession in general. Librarianship is a White, female-dominated profession, which can create a challenge when attempting to recruit and retain people of color but more specifically Black male librarians. There is a gap in understanding the professional, personal, and cultural challenges of minorities in majority-White professions.

BUILDING BRIDGES

Minority librarians often face difficult challenges and are the product of negative stereotyping, lack of understanding, and microaggressions that are subtly degrading. Increasing the diversity in librarianship requires bridging a gap to gain an understanding of the challenges that some minority librarians face in regard to professional identity. Too often, minority librarians find themselves in environments where their professionalism and experience are questioned because they are targets of invalidation and exclusion, accompanied by stereotyping based on their cultural, ethnic, and racial identities (Visconti, 2015). Throughout their careers, minorities have had to live in stealth and hide certain vilified aspects of their culture and identity in favor of those that are more palatable with regard to race and ethnicity (Visconti, 2015). Colleagues and administrators in libraries have to understand that minorities often face burdens, stresses, and anxieties in their everyday professional lives because they may be the only member or part of a very small number of minority librarians in an organization where these challenges are often considered nonissues (Curry, 1994). In a predominantly White profession, minority librarians are confronted with the burden of constantly having to qualify themselves and their experiences as equal to their colleagues. Too often they are isolated professionally because of the underrepresentation while also having to overcome elements of elitism, ethnocentrism, racism, and microaggressions (Curry, 1994). For libraries to make effective change, it is not only the responsibility of minorities to advocate and make their voices heard in bridging the gaps of diversity and inclusion but also that of library administrators to make conscientious efforts to recruit and hire minorities and provide opportunities for professional growth, networking, and mentoring. Library colleagues who have a willingness to understand and address issues faced in the profession by minority librarians and professional associations actively recruiting minorities for membership and scholarship programs will further the progress in bridging the gap.

Age Gaps

As the library profession continues to evolve, the generational issues of the workforce are evolving, as well. The library profession is an aging one, and it is perhaps in the best interest of the profession to embrace new librarians who may span various generations. It will be vital for library managers to adapt their management styles to adjust to the millennials, Generation Y/ nexters, and Generation D librarians joining the profession because each generation presents new challenges and differences (Mosley, 2002). Understanding these generational differences will be key in how the new wave of librarians will be able to meet the diverse needs of the next generation of users. Embracing varying generations across the profession will encourage positive interaction in the library, fresh ideas, differing perspectives, enthusiasm, and inclusion of those from nontraditional backgrounds. Mosley (2002) states that the future generations are in an opportunistic position to introduce a more tolerable and acceptable profession in terms of diversity and inclusion so that the library is a better reflection of the population's ethnicity demographics.

Gender Gaps

Gender can be defined in many ways. *The American Heritage Science Dictionary* defines it as "the sex of an individual, male or female, based on reproductive anatomy" (Gender, n.d.), which is typically the way gender is described. However, some gender studies would argue that gender is what a person chooses it to be. As African American men, regarding gender, we understand the inequalities and prejudices given for reasons that are not fair. For example, a male student worker may be asked by a supervisor to move a table or chair because they deem that the female student worker may have a harder time with it. However, is this fair? In a library, books are sometimes heavy, and a male student worker may not always be available to help with handling them. On the flip side, gender discrimination could be demonstrated if only a female student worker is asked to help with decorating the library. What if a male student worker is into design and can do a better job? James V. Carmichael Jr., author of "Gender Issues in the Workplace: Male Librarians Tell Their Side," confirms this when he states, "A surprisingly large number of respondents complained about the nature of tasks they felt implicitly expected to perform because they are male—lifting and moving heavy objects being the most frequent complaint. Conversely, one librarian objected to being excluded from interior decorating decisions" (Carmichael, 1994, p. 227).

In the 21st century, we must make an effort to remove these presumptions from our belief systems. Though this may be difficult, we must work every day to mute these beliefs. We must also learn to understand the difference between racism and prejudice. Learning this distinction will make the difference that we are seeking in America. Will Smith was quoted as stating, "Everybody is prejudiced, everybody has their life experiences that make them prefer one thing over another. But racism is more than that. For someone that actually thinks their race is superior to you, I don't want to work for them, I don't want to work at that company" (Brown, 2015). This is similar to our beliefs of how we can deal with gender inequality in America. If we are honest with each other and realize that we inherently have beliefs in what a male or a female should do, then we can work daily to debunk those invalid theories and grow as a nation. But if we continue to perpetuate these mores in our daily lives, then we will continue to suffer.

Racial and Ethnic Gaps

Race and ethnicity have become the changing face of librarianship. As more opportunities are given to diverse candidates, the workforce in librarianship will become more diverse. However, we must persistently push the envelope to the forefront to continue to see growth, or things will go back to the status quo. For example, many African Americans and other minorities thought strides were made in racial issues in America when Barack Obama was elected as the first African American president. Though strides were made with this historic election, moving forward and not sitting on our laurels must always be the goal. We must continue to push the agenda of making sure that the face of librarianship is that of a diverse community. Library administrators who make hiring decisions must look at the total applicant pool, including candidates of all hues of Brown; those with dreads, locs, or tattoos; those with or without religious affiliations; those who are part of the LGBTQ community; and many other diverse groups.

WHAT DOES A CULTURALLY COMPETENT LIBRARY LOOK LIKE?

Since 1989 there has been a foundational definition of *cultural competence.* Over the years, many scholars or others in academia have put their own twist on the definition of *cultural competency* to make it fit their topic or needs. To be culturally competent, you must value diversity, understand when cultural issues are deemed appropriate to be acted upon, have institutional cultural knowledge, and so forth. In reference to work by Cross et al. (1994), the National Center for Cultural Competence states,

> "Cultural competence is a set of congruent behaviors, attitudes, and policies that come together in a system, agency or among professionals and enable that system, agency or those professions to work effectively in cross-cultural situations." The word *culture* is used because it implies the integrated pattern of human behavior that includes thoughts, communications, actions, customs, beliefs, values and institutions of a racial, ethnic, religious or social group. The word *competence* is used because it implies having the capacity to function effectively. Five essential elements contribute to a system's, institution's, or agency's ability to become more culturally competent which include: (1) Valuing diversity, (2) Having the capacity for cultural self-assessment, (3) Being conscious of the dynamics inherent when cultures interact, (4) Having institutionalized culture knowledge, (5) Having developed adaptations to service

delivery reflecting an understanding of cultural diversity. (National Center for
Cultural Competence, n.d.)

Cross et al. (1994) provides a great foundational definition of *cultural competency* for others to decipher, research, discuss, and learn from. Many different organizations, including the National Center for Cultural Competence,
have used definition from Cross et al. (1994) as the groundwork to usher in
their own.

The National Center for Cultural Competence states that

> cultural competence requires that organizations: Have a defined set of values
> and principles, and demonstrate behaviors, attitudes, policies, and structures
> that enable them to work effectively cross-culturally. Have the capacity to (1)
> value diversity, (2) conduct self-assessment, (3) manage the dynamics of dif-
> ference, (4) acquire and institutionalize cultural knowledge, and (5) adapt to
> diversity and the cultural contexts of communities they serve. Incorporate the
> above in all aspects of policy-making, administration, practice and service
> delivery, systematically involve consumers, families and communities. Cultu-
> ral competence is a developmental process that evolves over an extended
> period. Both individuals and organizations are at various levels of awareness,
> knowledge and skills along the cultural competence continuum. (National
> Center for Cultural Competence, n.d.)

The National Alliance for Hispanic Health and the National Medical Association also have definitions of *cultural competence* that are derived from the
foundational definition by Cross et al. The National Alliance for Hispanic
Health states, "Cultural proficiency is when providers and systems seek to do
more than provide unbiased care as they value the positive role culture can
play in a person's health and well-being" (National Center for Cultural Competence, n.d.).

It is very important for libraries, banks, hospitals, and other public places
to be culturally proficient so users of these services will have positive cultural experiences. Whenever there is a negative experience, there is a chance
that the patron or customer may never use the service again. The National
Medical Association states that "Cultural Competency (Health) is the application of cultural knowledge, behaviors, and interpersonal and clinical skills
that enhances a provider's effectiveness in managing patient care" (National
Center for Cultural Competence, n.d.). Cultural competence is particularly
important in managing care. A culturally competent health care provider in a
scenario where the patient speaks English as a second language, for example,
may be able to pick up on cultural cues that might be missed otherwise.

STRATEGIC DIVERSITY

Diversity efforts in the library profession have missed the mark across several decades. The concept of diversity has often been lost due to questionable discussions of the need and purpose of it, uncommitted attempts at implementation, and dismissal of whether it's even an issue. To help push the diversity and inclusion movement forward, it is critical that libraries move away from just talking points for administrative presentations and instances of tokenism to intentionally employ strategic diversity efforts. Boisse and Dowell (1987) assert that, as far back as the late '80s and early '90s, the profession has been interested in recruiting qualified minorities but, as a whole, has put very little concentrated effort into following that interest with effective recruitment and opportunities. Kumaran (2015) states that it is important for libraries to cast a wide net to recruit and retain minorities who are visible and fight the urge to recruit those who resemble one's own image. Recruitment must first start early and continue through to library school. Strategic diversity necessitates that administrators support minorities with opportunities to lead, access to networks, constructive feedback, and mentorship. It also fosters an environment that allows minorities to be their authentic selves without feeling isolated or having to hide their cultural and racial identities to fit in or be accepted.

Mi and Zhang (2017) identify health sciences librarianship as an environment where diversity in the workforce is lacking and should seek to implement strategies to recruit graduates and librarians from underrepresented populations. This is supported by their study, which found that demographics of the health sciences workforce lacked diversity based on age and race. It is important for the library profession to take a "critical look at its culture, practices, and assumptions" in order to identify why minorities have barriers to entering the profession do not want to enter the profession, or do not stay with the profession (Mi & Zhang, 2017). What can libraries practically do to be strategic?

- Begin by developing an actionable minority recruitment plan.
- Be intentional about awareness and recruitment.
- Be willing to have uncomfortable conversations among library leadership and colleagues.
- Listen intently to what minorities share as needs.
- Take action, and move beyond talking to making effective changes.

CONCLUSION

In an ideal world, diversity in librarianship would not be an issue. There would be a melting pot of librarians of varying backgrounds, ethnicities, cultures, religions, races, genders, ages, and physical abilities. This diversity would be an accurate reflection of the communities and patrons whom we serve. This chapter identifies some areas of diversity that should be considered as libraries strive to move forward as a diverse entity and stay current with changing expectations. Diversity must continue to be at the forefront of library and library school strategic growth initiatives. "A culturally diverse library environment is its own best marketing tool to attract diverse groups to the library and to librarianship" (Chadley, 1992, p. 212).

As librarians we invest a lot of time and resources into understanding and discussing how libraries benefit our users and what resources they need. Cultivating a positive user experience and making them feel welcome are also a part of that investment, but many of our minority colleagues do not feel that same commitment of being welcomed, valued, or included. Not all hope is lost. Diversity is still an attainable goal. Hastings (2015) states that building an inclusive, diverse environment is never finished, as there are no quotas to fill, but when everyone has a voice and the opportunity to share their thoughts, it is good.

REFERENCES

Abdullahi, I., & Josey, E. J. (2002). Why diversity in American libraries. *Library Management,23*(1/2), 10–16. Retrieved from https://doi.org/10.1108/01435120210413544

Boisse, J. A., & Dowell, C. V. (1987). Increasing minority librarians in academic research libraries. *Library Journal, 112*(7), 52–54.

Brown, N. (2015). "Will Smith says he lives with prejudice, but racism is rare." Retrieved from http://www.msnbc.com/msnbc/will-smith-says-he-lives-prejudice-racism-rare

Carmichael, J. (1994). Gender issues in the workplace: Male librarians tell their side. *American Libraries, 25*(3), 227–230. Retrieved from http://www.jstor.org/stable/25633191

Chadley, O. A. (1992). Addressing cultural diversity in academic and research libraries. *College and Research Libraries, 53*(3), 206–214.

Curry, D. A. (1994). Your worries ain't like mine: African American librarians and the pervasiveness of racism, prejudice and discrimination in academe. *Reference Librarian, 21*(45–46), 299–311.

Gender. (n.d.). In *The American Heritage Science Dictionary*. Retrieved from http://www.dictionary.com/browse/gender

Hastings, S. K. (2015). If diversity is a natural state, why don't our libraries mirror the populations they serve? *Library Quarterly, 85*(2), 133. Retrieved from https://doi.org/10.1086/680152

Hathcock, A. (2015). White librarianship in blackface: Diversity initiatives in LIS. *In the Library With the Lead Pipe*. Retrieved from http://www.inthelibrarywiththeleadpipe.org/2015/lis-diversity/

Hudson-Ward, A. (2014). Eyeing the new diversity. *American Libraries, 45*(7/8), 32–35.

Kelley, M. (2013). Diversity never happens: The story of minority hiring doesn't seem to change much | Editorial. *Library Journal*. Retrieved from http://lj.libraryjournal.com/2013/

02/opinion/editorial/diversity-never-happens-the-story-of-minority-hiring-doesnt-seem-to-change-much/

Kumaran, M. (2015). Succession planning process that includes visible minority librarians. *Library Management, 36*(6/7), 434–447.

Mi, M., & Zhang, Y. (2017). Culturally competent library services and related factors among health sciences librarians: An exploratory study. *Journal of the Medical Library Association: JMLA, 105*(2), 132.

Mosley, P. A. (2002). Shedding the stereotypes. *Reference Librarian, 37*(78), 167–176.

National Center for Cultural Competence. (n.d.). Definitions of cultural competence: A project of the National Center for Cultural Competence. Retrieved from https://nccc.georgetown.edu/curricula/culturalcompetence.html

Visconti, G. (2015). Legislation without empathy: Race and ethnicity in LIS. *Partnership: The Canadian Journal of Library and Information Practice and Research, 10*(2), 1.

Chapter Four

Implicit Bias and Microaggressions in Library and Information Science

Nicole A. Cooke and Miriam E. Sweeney

You know the fury that comes over you when you're affected by other people's prejudice? The coldness, shock, or devastation when they put you or your loved ones down over race, sexual orientation, age, gender, size, class or ability? Maybe you felt it when your folks wouldn't let you bring your partner to a family celebration, when a white woman crashed your MLK event to announce that she deals with racism too, or when a classmate blocked your path to stare at your walking aid. Despite what a lot of defensive apologists might try to tell you, these incidents do matter: They're called microaggressions.

—Deb Jannerson

THE ELEPHANT IN THE ROOM

In the parable of the "Blind Men and the Elephant" by Rumi (1925), a group of blind men are presented with an elephant, and not knowing what it was, they decided to feel the elephant to determine what it was. Each man felt a different part of the elephant and came to their own conclusions as to what the creature was. For example, the man who felt the tail declared that he felt a rope, and the man who felt the elephant's side thought he had run into a wall. Each of the blind men had their own partial determinations and perceptions of the elephant, and none of them could identify the animal for what it was. This story, which appears in Buddhist, Hindu, and Jain religious texts, is used to demonstrate the subjectivity and range of "truth" and experiences and is an example of how people use their partial truths to define the world around them. Such is what we encounter with implicit biases, which can then manifest as microaggressions in interpersonal interactions. Humans instinctively project their partial understandings and opinions onto the world around them. Sometimes this internal sense-making is correct, and other times, like the blind men, internal sense-making falls short and leaves us with an incomplete and incorrect view of our surroundings.

Also known as implicit social cognition, *implicit bias* refers to the internal attitudes or stereotypes that affect our understanding, actions, and decisions in an unconscious manner (Kirwan Institute, n.d.). We acquire implicit biases and stereotypes through socialization, and these are the ways in which our minds categorize and attempt to make sense of people, things, and situations—they guide our interaction with the world. These beliefs can be positive or negative, implicit and then explicit. These beliefs are entrenched and hard to dismiss or replace, even when we recognize that they are false or harmful to others. Another dimension of implicit bias is that it encourages us to view groups as true representations of the individuals within the group. Banaji and Greenwald (2016) state that "we fail to perceive individuals as individuals. They are often viewed as representatives of social groups" (p. 17). Even when presented with contrary information, we resist changing long-held beliefs because it is easier to make a sweeping generalization than to decipher and reconcile the nuances and complexities of the individuals contained within any given group. For example, homeless people are often characterized as jobless, disheveled, and odiferous; however, many homeless people are clean and neat, just as there are employed and housed individuals who lack hygiene and grooming habits.

Banaji and Greenwald (2016) further extend the notion of implicit bias and stereotypes by referring to them as social mindbugs, which are "perceptions that affect our understanding of reactions to our own identities," particularly before *we* become members of said groups (p. 6). The mindbugs direct our thinking about groups (e.g., all senior citizens are cranky and hard of hearing) and prevent us from recognizing individuals in these groups (e.g., the senior who is a triathlete or bodybuilder). This can lead to cognitive dissonance because surely we will not be like that once we become members of the group. Consider these all-too-familiar defensive statements: "I'm not racist because I have a Black friend" or "I'm not xenophobic because there's a Muslim family in my neighborhood." Implicit biases, stereotypes, and social mindbugs thrive on automatic responses and perceptions of groups that are different from and don't apply to us as individuals. If we can be cognizant and reflective about our thoughts and responses, we can attempt to move past harmful and socialized knee-jerk reactions to people who are different. Just like the blind men and their misconceptions about the elephant, our partial perceptions and beliefs are not representative of whole groups, and we need to consider the larger context and recognize all of the pieces of a puzzle before making determinations.

IMPLICIT BIASES AND STEREOTYPES IN SOCIETY

There are any number of examples of implicit bias in our everyday lives, inside and outside of our libraries. In the 1940s, Drs. Kenneth and Mamie Clark conducted the doll experiment, which exposed the implicit racial biases held by children. When Black children were presented with two dolls, one White and one Black, 63% of the children selected the White doll to play with because they thought the White doll was "nicer," "prettier," and "cleaner" than the Black doll. In a replication of the study conducted in 2009, similar results occurred, with one young Black girl rejecting the Black doll, saying, "It talks back and don't follow directions" (Ahuja, 2009). Similar sentiments arise in online searches; for example, when a search for unprofessional hair was typed into Google, a predominance of images of Black women, many with natural hair, were returned (Alexander, 2016). Is Google racist, or are the codes behind the search engines just reflecting the biases and stereotypes of larger society? Other examples of how implicit biases manifest in society include the plethora of racist Halloween costumes that appear every October (Kai-Hwa Wang, 2016) and public-service campaigns attempting to disrupt the model minority stereotype by explicating the fact that not all Asian and Pacific Islanders are the same (APIASF, 2018). Implicit biases and stereotyping can indeed become explicit and systemic and lead to prejudice or negative perceived judgments about groups of people. The application of these prejudices to individuals or groups (microaggressions) can result in personal and social damage.

A THOUSAND TINY CUTS

Pierce (1970) coined the term *microaggressions* to refer to "subtle, stunning, often automatic, and non-verbal exchanges which are 'put downs'" (Pierce, Carew, Pierce-Gonzalez, & Willis, 1978, p. 66). These exchanges are often directed at minorities, reflecting external expressions of unrecognized internal bias, as well as expressions of explicit, conscious bias. Sue (2010) describes microaggressions as "commonplace daily verbal, behavioral, and environmental indignities, whether intentional or unintentional, that communicate hostile, derogatory, or negative slights" against the target group or individual. Microaggressions may be levied against a group or individual on the basis of race, ethnicity, gender expression, sexual orientation, or ability (to name but a few vectors), often in intersectional ways that engage interlocking identities simultaneously. In this sense, microaggressions function as manifestations of broader societal power dynamics, reinforcing positions of power and privilege at the interpersonal level.

Sue et al. (2007, p. 278) propose a taxonomy of racial microaggressions that detail the variant forms and manifestations of these interactions: *Micro-insults* (often unconscious "behavioral/verbal remarks or comments that convey rudeness, insensitivity"); *microassaults* (conscious "explicit racial derogations characterized primarily by a violent verbal or nonverbal attack meant to hurt the intended victim through name-calling, avoidant behavior or purposeful discriminatory actions"); and *microinvalidations* (unconscious "verbal comments or behaviors that exclude, negate, or nullify the psychological thoughts, feelings, or experiential reality of a person of color"). Examples of common racial microaggressions might include comments that assume foreignness of non-White Americans (e.g., "Where were you born?"), ascriptions of intelligence based on race (e.g., "You are so articulate"), or assumptions of criminality of people of color (e.g., a store owner following a customer of color around the store; Sue et al., 2007, p. 276). These examples communicate racial slights, assumptions of otherness, and inferiority of people of color.

Microaggressions are often subtle and therefore may go unrecognized, particularly by those in positions of power and privilege. Indeed, Sue (2005) notes that "the power of racial microaggressions lies in their invisibility to the perpetrator and, oftentimes, the recipient," who is left to parse the dynamics of a surprisingly or unexpected negative interaction after the fact. The covert nature of these slights can make microaggressions difficult to document and can contribute to negative workplace and educational environments for minority groups. Like a death by a thousand tiny cuts, the small indignities of microaggressions add up over time to cumulative harm, fatigue, and damage to recipients. Studies have shown that the effects of racial microaggressions have been linked to negative physical and mental health outcomes (Nadal et al., 2014; O'Keefe et al., 2015; Solórzano, Ceja, & Yosso, 2000), underscoring the severity of these interactions for minorities.

IMPLICIT BIAS AND MICROAGGRESSIONS IN LIS: LIS IS NOT IMMUNE

Library and information science (LIS) is not exempt from the effects of implicit bias and microaggressions. For instance, a study investigating a wide range of racial discrimination across a range of public services in the United States found that, for public libraries surveyed, "emails signed with a distinctively African American name are less likely to receive a reply than identical emails signed with a distinctively white name" (Giulietti, Tonin, & Vlassopoulos, 2015). Libraries serve an array of diverse communities with a variety of backgrounds, life experiences, and needs. Given that librarianship is overwhelmingly dominated by White, middle-class, and able-bodied women

(American Library Association, 2012), it is particularly important to consider how implicit bias and microaggressions may shape library services, policies, practices, and interpersonal interactions between coworkers and patrons alike.

Microaggressions particularly have become a topic of interest in the LIS community. Conferences and professionally sponsored events on microaggressions have been featured at the annual meetings of the Library Leadership and Management Association (LLAMA), the American Library Association (ALA), and the Public Library Association (PLA) over the last few years (e.g., Moore & Alabi, 2015; Anderson, Young, & King, 2016). The library community has also taken to the Internet to share stories and raise awareness about the impacts of microaggressions in LIS. For instance, the critical library, or "critlib," movement has hosted scheduled Twitter discussions to talk about microaggressions and related issues using a combination of the hashtags #critlib and #microaggressions or to aggregate the conversations in public Twitter feeds (http://critlib.org). The website Microaggressions in Librarianship collects and shares anonymous submissions about people's experiences in the LIS profession (http://lismicroaggressions.tumblr.com/about). Examples shared on the site reveal the range of microaggressions experienced by library professionals and students, demonstrating the pervasiveness of these encounters and their impacts on the recipients. One submission notes, "I have been called 'ethnic,' 'exotic,' and 'festive' by my coworkers. I've also been asked if 'I'm something,' with something meaning a race other than white." Documenting these encounters makes them visible and, in doing so, creates opportunities for validation and potential for intervention.

The experiences described on the Microaggressions in Librarianship website are reflected in research that suggests microaggressions function as a persistent feature of the LIS workplace (Alabi, 2015). Alabi's (2015) investigation of academic librarians' experiences with racial microaggressions in the workplace found that racial minority librarians regularly experience racial microaggressions directed at them from their nonminority colleagues. This study also determined that nonminority librarians were far less likely to report observing microaggressions in the workplace, highlighting the disconnect of experiences between racial minority librarians and nonminorities within the same work environments. This raises important questions about the role of implicit bias and microaggressions in shaping unwelcome LIS professional environments for people of color and minorities.

ADDRESSING IMPLICIT BIAS AND MICROAGGRESSIONS IN LIS

Addressing implicit bias and microaggressions in LIS requires familiarity not only with these specific concepts but also more generally with structures of power and privilege in society. Our (Sweeney & Cooke, 2018) study of an online discussion thread about microaggressions in a social media group for LIS professionals revealed multiple and conflicting (mis)understandings of what microaggressions are and how they function as interpersonal expressions of power. Many participants in the thread discussed microaggressions as individual instances of personal offense, with recipients of microaggressions positioned as being "overly sensitive," rather than as expressions of implicit bias shaped by broader structures of inequality. We argue that the failure of the participants to locate microaggressions in a context of societal power foreclosed the potential of the discussion thread to properly validate the experiences of those who encounter microaggressions (often people from marginalized groups) and formed strategies for disrupting these harmful interactions in the LIS classroom and workplace.

So, what should we do about implicit bias? How do we identify and disrupt harmful microaggressions? Multivalent efforts across LIS education, professional development, institutional structures, and individual awareness can all contribute to shifting the landscape of our profession toward equality and inclusion. We (Sweeney & Cooke, 2018) encourage LIS educators to actively teach about microaggressions in the context of power and privilege as a key component of training future library professionals. Conscious development of empathy, cultural competence, and building an awareness of positionality are part and parcel of the success of these conversations. Additionally, institutional policies and workplace norms should be examined for potential bias and embedded negative assumptions. ALA suggests six steps for changing bias in the workplace that emphasize active reflection and engagement with implicit bias as a key part of professional practice (http://www.ala.org/advocacy/diversity/workplace/diversityplanning). Such resources such as Harvard's Project Implicit (https://implicit.harvard.edu/implicit) can serve as useful tools to spawn these conversations and aid in reflection. These strategies, when mobilized together, begin to bring implicit bias and microaggressions, the elephants in the room, more clearly into focus.

REFERENCES

Ahuja, G. (2009, March 31). What a doll tells us about race. Retrieved from http://abc news.go.com/GMA/story?id=7213714

Alabi, J. (2015). Racial microaggressions in academic libraries: Results of a survey of minority and non-minority librarians. *Journal of Academic Librarianship, 41*, 47–53.

Alexander, L. (2016, April 8). Do Google's "unprofessional hair" results show it is racist? *Guardian.* Retrieved from https://www.theguardian.com/technology/2016/apr/08/does-goo gle-unprofessional-hair-results-prove-algorithms-racist-

American Library Association. (2012). *Diversity counts.* Retrieved from http://www.ala.org/ offices/diversity/diversitycounts/divcounts

Anderson, M., Young, K., & King, K. (2016, April 5–9). Understanding microaggressions: A catalyst for climate change in the workplace. Presented at the meeting of the Public Library Association, Denver, Colorado.

Asian and Pacific Islander American Scholarship Fund (APIASF). (2018). I am #NotTheSame. Retrieved from http://www.wearenotthesame.org/

Banaji, M. R., & Greenwald, A. G. (2016). *Blindspot: Hidden biases of good people.* New York: Bantam.

Giulietti, C., Tonin, M., & Vlassopoulos, M. (2015). Racial discrimination in local public services: A field experiment in the United States. CESifo Working Paper No. 5537, Center for Economic Studies and Ifo Institute (CESifo), Munich. Retrieved from https:// www.econstor.eu/bitstream/10419/123178/1/cesifo_wp5537.pdf

Jannerson, D. (2011, April 14). Microaggressions: Because it is a big deal. *Bitch Magazine.* Retrieved from https://www.bitchmedia.org/post/microaggressions-because-it-IS-a-big-deal

Kai-Hwa Wang, F. (2016, October 27). Student campaign fights "culturally appropriative" Halloween costumes. Retrieved from https://www.nbcnews.com/news/asian-america/stu dent-campaign-fights-against-culturally-appropriative-halloween-costumes-n673546

Kirwan Institute for the Study of Race and Ethnicity at the Ohio State University. (n.d.). Understanding implicit bias. Retrieved from http://kirwaninstitute.osu.edu/research/under standing-implicit-bias/

Moore, A. A., & Alabi, J. (2015, March 18). Racial and LGBT microaggressions: An introduc- tion for library leaders [Webinar]. In *Library Leadership and Management Association webinar series.* Retrieved from http://connect.ala.org/node/236056

Nadal, K. L., Griffin, K. E., Wong, Y., Hamit, S., & Rasmus, M. (2014). The impact of racial microaggressions on mental health: Counseling implications for clients of color. *Journal of Counseling and Development, 92,* 57–66.

O'Keefe, V. M., Wingate, L. R., Cole, A. B., Hollingsworth, D. W., & Tucker, R. P. (2015). Seemingly harmless racial communications are not so harmless: Racial microaggressions lead to suicidal ideation by way of depression symptoms. *Suicide and Life-Threatening Behavior, 45*(5), 567–576.

Pierce, C. (1970). Offensive mechanisms. In F. Barbour (Ed.), *The Black seventies* (pp. 265–282). Boston: Porter Sargent.

Pierce, C., Carew, J. V., Pierce-Gonzalez, D., & Willis, D. (1978). An experiment in racism: TV commercials. In C. Pierce (Ed.), *Television and education* (pp. 62–88). Beverly Hills, CA: Sage.

Rumi, G. A. D. (1925). *The Mathnawí of Jalálu'ddín Rúmí.* New Delhi, India: Adam.

Solórzano, D., Ceja, M., & Yosso, T. (2000, Winter). Critical race theory, racial microaggres- sions, and campus racial climate: The experiences of African American college students. *Journal of Negro Education, 69,* 60–73.

Sue, D. W. (2005). Racism and the conspiracy of silence. *Counseling Psychologist, 33,* 100–114.

Sue, D. W. (2010). *Microaggressions in everyday life: Race, gender, and sexual orientation.* Wiley.

Sue, D. W., Capodilupo, C. M., Torino, G. C., Bucceri, J. M., Holder, A. M. B., Nadal, K. L., & Esquilin, M. (2007). Racial microaggressions in everyday life: Implications for clinical practice. *American Psychologist, 62,* 271–286.

Sweeney, M. E., & Cooke, N. A. (2018). You're so sensitive! How LIS professionals define and discuss microaggressions online. *Library Quarterly: Information, Community, Policy, 88*(4), 375–390.

Chapter Five

Subversive Librarianship as a Strategy for Social Justice and Activism

Rebecca Hankins

> I really didn't realize the librarians were, you know, such a dangerous group. They are subversive. You think they're just sitting there at the desk, all quiet and everything. They're like plotting the revolution.
>
> —Michael Moore

The word *subversion* has many meanings, but the definition most often understood connects it to government and politics. Globally governments have considered any type of subversive activities as treasonous and worthy of jailing and even death. Often it has been used to maintain control and stamp out any dissent, even in the United States. *Subversive activity* has been defined by the U.S. Department of Defense as

> anyone lending aid, comfort, and moral support to individuals, groups, or organizations that advocate the overthrow of incumbent governments by force and violence is subversive and is engaged in subversive activity. All willful acts that are intended to be detrimental to the best interests of the government and that do not fall into the categories of treason, sedition, sabotage, or espionage will be placed in the category of subversive activity. (U.S. Department of Defense, 2010, p. 351)

The reaction to the end of slavery was to find subversive ways to reenslave the newly freed population: "Southern state governments worked openly to pass the legal mechanisms that criminalized blackness and poverty, from black codes and apprenticeships laws to vagrancy provisions and convict lease systems" (Rael, 2016). Similarly, terror lynching (distinguished from other racialized violence) was a subversion of the American justice system. As the Equal Justice Initiative notes, these public-spectacle lynchings "were attended by the entire white community and conducted as celebratory acts of racial control and domination. These activities resulted in one of this country's largest mass migrations of one group, African Americans, from the Deep South to northern states to escape racism, extreme violence, and oppression" (Equal Justice Initiative, 2018, p. 6).

The United States has had a number of periods in its history that we now view as shameful and shockingly normalized throughout government systems (legislative and penal), including the creation of the "House Un-American Activities Committee formed in 1938 to investigate alleged disloyalty and subversive activities on the part of private citizens, public employees, and those organizations suspected of having Communist ties" (Subversion, 2018). This led to the horrific blacklisting of actors, writers, and the film industry during the Joseph McCarthy hearings of the 1950s. The impulses of governments to maintain control by any means necessary has always been met by those who have often had to resort to subversive activities and tools to challenge oppressive systems. Whistleblowers have used their positions and visibility to expose illegal and deadly activities of the U.S. government, including the release of the Pentagon papers by Daniel Ellsberg to the *Washington Post* and the video leaks of Iraqi massacres and diplomatic cables by army intelligence analyst Chelsea Manning. These can all fall under the rubric of subversive activities that we would not have known about had it not been for individuals putting their careers and lives on the line. History tells us that individuals and actions that appear in the past as negatively subversive often appear heroic when looked at from a future perspective.

Globally, subversive behavior has also long been used as a mechanism by those oppressed to exact change and push against exclusionary practices. Even during the precarious era of slavery in the Americas, Africans would employ subversive tactics to maintain some semblance of humanity and defiance. "Subversive acts included sabotage of machinery, withholding labour as far as they dared, and renaming fellow enslaved Africans to ensure they kept their identity" (Real Histories Directory, n.d.). We should also recognize that those Africans, "forcibly captured and intended for a life of harsh servitude on American plantations" (Hiott, 2015, p. 2) often chose to jump to their deaths from transatlantic ships to avoid being enslaved. By this action, they were also subverting the system and taking control of their bodies and humanity. We also saw this in the work of the Black Panther Party's (BPP) use of the Second Amendment as a means of self-defense. The BPP's actions led to gun-control measures that would be unprecedented in these times of National Rifle Association (NRA) supremacy (Love, 2013). There has always been backlash when the oppressed have used methods that were meant to exclude them. All of these actions and reactions have encouraged others to push against the system in more and more creative ways.

Taking up the mantle of subversion has been a long tradition for performance and literary artists, filmmakers, television, and fiction writers, to name a few. For contemporary artists, Stephen Colbert is a celebrated satirist whose work has constantly subverted our notions of American conservative personalities and politics by his parody character performances. It must be noted that Colbert worked in Northwestern University's library, correcting computer data, so we may need to check those records! Also of note is that the Colbert Education Center and Library Building, which houses the Medical University of South Carolina (MUSC) Libraries, is named after Stephen Colbert's father, James William Colbert Jr., the first vice president of academic affairs at MUSC.

INSPIRATIONAL WORKS

Why is it necessary to be subversive? This chapter expands on the use of subversive behavior to interrogate the profession of librarianship and how it is necessary to subvert the norms in order to achieve social justice and agency. It also builds on the work of a number of recent publications by librarians and archivists, including the two-volume *Critical Library Pedagogy Handbook* that "questions the ethics and morality of defining learning through needs set by the marketplace and an uncritical questioning of the status quo" (Pagowsky & McElroy, 2016, p. ix). The 2017 publication *Librarians With Spines* also "pushes the boundaries of social justice community service, library and information science, equitable bibliographic taxonomy, and ubiquitous information literacy" (Macias et al., 2017).

Geoff Walton's (2017) essay "Information Literacy Is a Subversive Activity: Developing a Research-Based Theory of Information Discernment" was one of the few articles that had *subversive* in its title. Very much worth the read, it ultimately theorizes how information literacy can be used to subvert preconceived notions of learning abilities and styles. Short-term exposure to information literacy concepts had significant impact on students' abilities to question, discern, analyze, and evaluate information more effectively, but there is a need to go beyond this to "minimize their tendency towards confirmation bias and motivated reasoning so that they can reach the highest order of information discernment" (Walton, 2017, p. 152).

These and other works seek to empower and provoke librarians to move out of their comfort zones and challenge the prevailing morass that affects the library profession. This chapter discusses different methods used by librarians to save libraries, push for diversity within the profession, and bring public awareness to support social justice. These survival tools and strategies for the library field impart knowledge on how to affect change on a large or small scale.

SAVING INTERNATIONAL AND NATIONAL LIBRARIES

Rarely do we look at librarians as heroes, but there have been some heroic stories of librarians who have used their skills to subvert and ultimately save libraries, allowing the profession to be held up as a model for the world. Three instances of this heroic nature are exemplified in the librarians of Timbuktu Mali, the National Library of Iraq, and the four Connecticut librarians who fought the U.S. government regarding the Patriot Act. These examples show that standing up is not always rewarded with applause, but it can always inspire others to do the right thing.

Timbuktu Librarians

Although there have been some tragic deaths of librarians in the United States, mostly due to domestic violence, rarely is that a concern in the librarian work environment. Librarians in public library environments do tend to face more instances of assault, harassment, and dealing with challenging patrons. But even in these environments, librarians can call on security to help handle difficult encounters. Librarians around the world, on the other hand, have often found their lives in danger, where death or imprisonment is a real possibility. None more so than the librarians who saved manuscript documents and other rare materials from 2012 to 2014 in Mali. In fact, if one views the list of UNESCO World Heritage in Danger, the majority of the properties listed as threatened by serious and specific dangers are in Africa (UNESCO World Heritage Centre, n.d.).

Mali is known for its amazing mosques and residential architecture built from sculptured sand dunes. In 2012, an Al-Qaida-affiliated group decided that it would embark on a campaign to destroy the historic mud cities in Mali. Abdel Kader Haidara, a young Malian scholar-librarian and resident of Timbuktu, had amassed a library of close to 400,000 rare manuscripts and documents. He had convinced his fellow Malians that he would conserve and preserve this history of Timbuktu and Mali's legacy. In 2011, he and others saw the tides of severe and un-Islamic practices sweeping the government and many Sufi shrines being destroyed. Haidara and his colleagues began a process of hiding and concealing manuscripts to remove them from the endangered areas to ship them to Bamako, Mali. Eventually having to use boats on the Niger River, "the manuscripts were loaded in pinnaces—30-foot-long watercraft—each carrying 15 metal chests filled with manuscripts" (Glenn, 2016). These selfless and dangerous acts are summed up by Hammer (2017), who wrote, "Timbuktu had been the incubator for the richness of Islam and Islam in its perverted form had attempted to destroy it. But the original power of the culture itself, and the people, like Haidara . . . had saved the great manuscripts in the end" (p. 212).

Iraq National Libraries

When the United States invaded Iraq in 2003, there was long-term destruction, looting, and damage to Iraq's cultural institutions. When newspapers blared headlines of the loss and devastation to Iraq's cultural history, some thought it would never be the same, and they were correct. The longtime director of the National Library of Iraq, Saad Eskander, faced scorn, lawsuits, and character assassination since he had vocally protested the damage done to the libraries and cultural institutions in Iraq. In an *American Libraries Magazine* interview, Eskander talked about his staff and how dealing with their emotions was a priority: "Even the staff of the Iraqi Library was totally demoralized by the looting and the destruction of their institution. So my first effort was to restore their self-confidence and make them believe that they could rebuild the National Library step-by-step" (Kniffel, 2007). The fact that Eskander understood how important it was to start with his staff was a subversive act, especially in a place where colleagues had been killed or kidnapped and where war raged on. Acknowledging the importance of the staff during this period took courage and selflessness beyond mere duty to the state. At the dedication of the new Baghdad Library scheduled to be built in 2013, Eskander noted, "It is imperative for the new Iraq to consolidate its young democracy and good governance through knowledge. New libraries have a notable role to play by promoting unconditional access to information, freedom of expression, cultural diversity, and transparency. By responding to the needs of Iraq's next generations, the new library, we hope, will play an important role in the future of our country" (Griffiths, 2014).

Connecticut Librarians

In the aftermath of the 9/11 terrorist acts, the U.S. government passed the Patriot Act in 2001 that allowed the FBI to drastically increase what was called "national security letters (NSL)" that were previously used to gather foreign intelligence but not used on American citizens. The most troubling aspect of the increased use of NSL was the gag order attached to these letters, prohibiting libraries from informing patrons that they were the subject of these orders or from publicizing any aspect of the transaction. Four Connecticut librarians fought this law and were ultimately successful in showing "the entire nsl provision of the Patriot Act was unconstitutional" (Goodman, 2017). These librarians stood up and chose to fight and subvert the system, which has had an impact on all libraries and librarians throughout this country.

DIVERSIFYING THE PROFESSION: GROWING OUR OWN

Recruitment of a diverse workforce in libraries has been an ongoing struggle. Some of the subversive methods used for recruitment include growing one's own, writing about the profession through journals and books, developing YouTube videos, and moving into public activism. There are a number of successful "Grow Your Own" programming grants via the Institute of Museum and Library Services (IMLS) and American Library Association (ALA) that are specifically for the recruitment and training of Native Americans and students at Hispanic-serving institutions and historic Black colleges and universities (IMLS, n.d.). These are continuing programs that have been funded for many years, but unfortunately none of this funding targets the K–12 audience. There needs to be a strategic initiative that focuses on the recruitment and educational programming for K–12 to tap into those connections as recruits for future library professionals. There are similar programs for health, engineering, and other disciplinary professions. Since the library touches almost every child in America, either in the public or in the school library venue, our profession is staring a missed strategic opportunity right in the face. In an effort to recruit a new and diverse workforce for the future, let's use these connections to the K–12 audience to promote the profession while students are formulating their future careers.

LIBRARIANS AND SOCIAL JUSTICE

The library and archival worlds have been writing and pushing social justice for a long time and are just now getting the publicity and acknowledgment they deserve. There is a long history of social justice critique within the library's cataloging and classification systems. Sanford Berman's publication of *Prejudices and Antipathies* was a particularly incisive critique of the Library of Congress (LC) subject headings nomenclature concerning people; the critique specifically called out the discriminatory terminology regarding race, religion, gender, and age (Berman, 1971). His critique led to many important and lasting changes to LC subject headings. Hope A. Olson's book *The Power to Name: Locating the Limits of Subject Representation in Libraries* also critiqued the Western-centric norms of classification (Olson, 2011).

Archival leader and former Society of American Archivist president Mark Greene argued in his article "A Critique of Social Justice as an Archival Imperative: What Is It We're Doing That's All That Important?" that archivists should not engage in social justice (Greene, 2013). Many others argue much more persuasively that all libraries and archives are political, and social justice should be in the forefront of what we collect. As David Wallace wrote, "Struggles for social justice are battlegrounds over values, priorities, resources, dignity, and survival. To claim that such initiatives politicize archives misses the point that archives are already political and always manifested and shaped at the coalface of power, privilege and resourcing" (Wallace, 2010, p. 184). Verne Harris similarly noted this in "The Archive Is Politics" from his book *Archives and Justice: A South African Perspective* (Harris, 2007). Archivists are taking on the mantle of social justice. In a thoughtful interview for the National Digital Stewardship Alliance titled "Archives Have Never Been Neutral," Jarrett Drake, archivist and scholar, challenges the archival profession to value liberational ideals that expand the notion of the profession and the work being done to be more diverse and inclusive (NDSA, 2017). Other writers are embracing social activism as it relates to our notions of who owns our history and interrogating our concepts of provenance (creators of records) versus those who determine what is historical. Geraci and Caswell's article "Developing a Typology of Human Rights Records" discusses these new challenges to our notion of ownership and power (Geraci & Caswell, 2016). When we talk about human rights, we must understand whose perspectives we are documenting from, who has the power to determine what is documented, and who determines what voices are heard or silenced.

There are a number of important works that push the profession toward social activism and promoting the public good. *Libraries, Human Rights, and Social Justice: Enabling Access and Promoting Inclusion* by Jaeger, Taylor, and Gorham (2015) very succinctly encourages librarians to be activists and change agents within their communities by engaging the public from their spaces rather than library spaces. Cox and Wallace's *Archives and the Public Good: Accountability and Records in Modern Society* looks at the responsibility that information professionals have to ensure that records are maintained and accessible. They argue that, though we all have inherent biases, we must put them aside as much as possible for the public good (Cox & Wallace, 2002). Verne Harris also noted in his book the need to document the good, the bad, and the ugly. Again, who decides what is important is political, and that should be acknowledged from the beginning (Harris, 2007).

Too often librarians and archivists have been told to just stay in their corners and serve the public because they have nothing to say or offer. However, recent writings and events have shown that librarians and archivists can take the forefront and make a difference. The Occupy Wall Street Library (n.d.) and the ongoing work of Righting the Record Oral History Project (People's Archive of Police Violence in Cleveland, n.d.) are two examples of strategic engagements by librarians and archivists in social activism and change that should be proudly remembered. Although the Occupy Wall Street activism was short-lived, the library documented the work of the activists, offering a service to thousands of individuals involved in the protest. Similarly, the Righting the Record Project assisted the community activists in interviewing and collecting stories of police violence in Cleveland.

CONCLUSION

This chapter makes it clear that there is a stark need for a corpus of research on social justice, activism, and community engagement within the library field. The professional, informational, and digital divide within the library and archival professions is worth discussion. There are many librarians and archivists leading the way, as showcased in this chapter. These groups and individuals are inspirational, but often they didn't choose to be activists or subversive; they rose to the occasion. There are many such examples of people doing the hard work and making the tough decisions. We need more of us within the information profession to push against the prevailing winds and try new ways of engaging the field and the public. Continue to share ideas that can be discussed widely, debated often, and made accessible in as many venues and resources as possible. Understanding the importance of addressing social justice within the profession allows for a more dynamic and engaged profession. The ultimate outcome is that subversive librarianship becomes the norm, and in so doing, we transform and extend the relevancy of our work.

REFERENCES

American Library Association (ALA). (n.d.). Knowledge river admissions. Retrieved December 27, 2018, from https://ischool.arizona.edu/knowledge-river-admissions

American Library Association (ALA). (n.d.). Spectrum scholarship. Retrieved December 27, 2018, from http://www.ala.org/awardsgrants/spectrum-scholarship &

Berman, S. (1971). *Prejudices and antipathies*. Jefferson, NC: McFarland.

Cox, R. J., & Wallace, D. A. (2002). *Archives and the public good: Accountability and records in modern society*. Westport, CT: Quorum Books.

Equal Justice Initiative. (2018). Lynching in America: Confronting the legacy of racial terror. Retrieved November 10, 2018, from https://eji.org/reports/lynching-in-america

Geraci, N., & Caswell, M. (2016). Developing a typology of human rights records. *Journal of Contemporary Archival Studies, 3*(1). Retrieved June 18, 2018, from https://elischo lar.library.yale.edu/jcas/vol3/iss1/1

Glenn, T. (2016, April 14). Review of *The bad-ass librarians of Timbuktu: And their race to save the world's most precious manuscripts* by J. Hammer. *Washington Independent Review of Books*. Retrieved November 10, 2018, from http://www.washingtoninde pendentreviewofbooks.com/bookreview/the-bad-ass-librarians-of-timbuktu-and-their-race-to-save-the-worlds-most-p

Goodman, D. (2017, June 27). America's most dangerous librarians. *Mother Jones*. Retrieved June 27, 2018, from https://www.motherjones.com/politics/2008/09/americas-most-danger ous-librarians/

Greene, M. (2013). A critique of social justice as an archival imperative: What is it we're doing that's all that important? *American Archivist, 76*(2), 302–334. doi:10.17723/aarc.76.2.147441214663kw43

Griffiths, A. (2014, August 27). Designs unveiled for new public library in Iraq. Retrieved November 24, 2018, from https://www.dezeen.com/2013/06/11/designs-unveiled-for-new-baghdad-library-by-ambs-architects/

Hammer, J. (2016). *The bad-ass librarians of Timbuktu and their race to save the world's most precious manuscripts.* New York: Simon & Schuster.

Harris, V. (2007). *Archives and justice: A South African perspective.* Chicago: Society of American Archivists.

Hoitt, S. G. et al. (2015) *My name is Omar: A life in the struggle for liberation.* Clemson, SC: Clemson University.

Institute of Museum and Library Services (IMLS). (n.d.). Laura Bush 21st century librarian program. Retrieved December 27, 2018, from https://www.imls.gov/grants/available/laura-bush-21st-century-librarian-program

Jaeger, P. T., Taylor, N. G., & Gorham, U. (2015). *Libraries, human rights, and social justice: Enabling access and promoting inclusion.* Lanham, MD: Rowman & Littlefield.

Kniffel, L. (2007, April 14). Interview with Iraq National Library director Saad Eskander. *American Libraries Magazine.* Retrieved November 10, 2018, from https://americanlibrariesmagazine.org/interview-with-iraq-national-library-director-saad-eskander/

Love, D. A. (2013, January 11). NRA was pro-gun control when it came to Black Panthers. Retrieved November 10, 2018, from https://thegrio.com/2013/01/11/nra-was-pro-gun-control-when-it-came-to-black-panthers/

Macias, M., et al. (2017). *Librarians with spines: Information agitators in an age of stagnation.* M. Macias and Y. S. Cura (Eds.). Los Angeles: Hinchas de Poesia Press.

National Digital Stewardship Alliance (NDSA). (2017, February 15). "Archives have never been neutral": An NDSA interview with Jarrett Drake. Retrieved November 10, 2018, from https://ndsa.org/2017/02/15/archives-have-never-been-neutral-an-ndsa-interview-with-jarrett-drake.html

Occupy Wall Street Library. (n.d.). Home page. Retrieved November 10, 2018, from https://peopleslibrary.wordpress.com/

Olson, H. A. (2011). *The power to name: Locating the limits of subject representation in libraries.* Dordrecht, Netherlands: Springer Netherlands.

Pagowsky, N., & McElroy, K. (Eds.). (2016). *Critical library pedagogy handbook.* Chicago: Association of College and Research Libraries.

A People's Archive of Police Violence in Cleveland. (n.d.). Righting the record oral history project. Retrieved November 10, 2018, from http://archivingpoliceviolence.org/collections/show/2

Rael, P. (2016, December 9). Demystifying the 13th Amendment and its impact on mass incarceration. Retrieved November 10, 2018, from https://www.aaihs.org/demystifying-the-13th-amendment-and-its-impact-on-mass-incarceration/

Real Histories Directory. (n.d.). The transatlantic slave trade. Retrieved from http://www.realhistories.org.uk/articles/archive/translantic-slave-trade

Subversion. (2018). In *Wikipedia.* Retrieved November 10, 2018, from https://en.wikipedia.org/wiki/Subversion

UNESCO World Heritage Centre. (n.d.). List of world heritage in danger. Retrieved November 24, 2018, from http://whc.unesco.org/en/danger/

U.S. Department of Defense, Joint Education and Doctrine Division. (2010, November). Dictionary of military and associated terms (as amended through 15 May 2011) [PDF]. *Joint Publication 1-02.*

Wallace, David A. (2010). Locating agency: Interdisciplinary perspectives on professional ethics and archival morality. *Journal of Information Ethics, 19*(1), 172–89.

Walton, G. G. (2017). Information literacy is a subversive activity: Developing a research-based theory of information discernment. *Journal of Information Literacy, 11*(1), 137–155.

Part II

Equipping the Library Staff

Chapter Six

Leading a Diverse and Inclusive Public Library

Cristina Dominguez Ramírez

You can lead a diverse and inclusive public library at any level and from any background.—Anjali Gulati

"Babies of Color Are Now the Majority, Census Says" was an *NPR Ed* blog headline on July 1, 2016 (Yoshinaga, 2016). At the time this chapter was written in 2018, the headline was just as important as it was then, if not more. It is especially relevant for librarians who serve increasingly diverse communities. In a climate where representation matters, front-line library personnel and library leaders typically do not represent the racial and ethnic makeup of the communities they serve. However, the need for inclusive library services and a diverse workforce is more important than ever before to meet the information-seeking needs of the communities served and to create positive learning spaces. "The bases for diversity efforts in organizations include awareness of the increasingly diverse population, as potential clients and potential hires, as well as addressing past inequities and current unfairness and eliminating underrepresentation" (Winston & Li, 2007).

Librarians of color and those identifying with underrepresented groups, for obvious reasons, have unique perspectives when it comes to designing library services, collections, programming, and outreach activities that are relevant and impactful for minority communities. Librarians identifying with underrepresented groups can imagine the difficulties for immigrant families trying to navigate their way through the American public education system and learning to use public libraries, especially if their native countries did not have many of these resources.

Diverse staff members can better relate to families who are looking for children's books that represent their skin tones, hair texture, and shared life experiences. They can also relate to patrons who feel excitement at fairs or outreach events that have a library staff member who looks like them or speaks their language. Based on my experience, when library staff members, managers, or leaders understand the community and create opportunities and resources for diverse communities to enjoy, the whole library can become a community hub, a third space of learning, engagement, and knowledge exchange.

The current demographics in librarianship indicate that most library managers, directors, and leaders are White. The percent of credentialed librarians who are White, according to the 2000 census, is 89%. The number of credentialed minority librarians is much smaller: 5% African American, 2% Latino, and less than 1% Native American (Davis & Hall, 2007). This chapter shares experiences, lessons learned, and challenges overcome while managing two libraries and beginning the journey on leading a third. This chapter may be of particular interest to public libraries. It is written for library personnel who want to lead at any level and see a need to create a more inclusive and diverse space in their libraries.

Urban Library

My first real leadership experience was at a library in an urban setting, and it was a type of baptism by fire. I had left academia and an academic library as a subject bibliographer and became the library community services manager for the Richmond Public Library's Broad Rock Branch. Located in central Virginia, the Richmond Public Library (RPL) consists of nine libraries serving the city of Richmond. RPL is an urban library system that has branches in neighborhoods across the city and serves a population of more than 220,000.

The Broad Rock Branch Library is located near the Hunter Holmes McGuire Veterans Administration Medical Center and serves a patron population that is largely African American, Hispanic/Latino, and Spanish speaking. The branch borders Chesterfield County, which has experienced a 234% growth in the Hispanic or Latino population from 2000 to 2015. All government services, especially K–12 schools and public libraries, have noticed the need to adapt and create services to better meet the needs of this rapidly growing community (Chesterfield County Planning Department, 2010). The median household income for the area is $37,189, which is lower than the median for Richmond at $42,373 (City-Data.com, 2017).

The Broad Rock Library's services include an after-school homework-help program that meets twice a week, story-time visits to local daycares, 24 public-access computers, as well as printing and faxing services. When I was hired, I immediately saw a great need to create services, collections, and resources for the Spanish-speaking/Latino community. A certified teacher from the Richmond Public School (RPS) system who was bilingual and a Latina organized the existing homework-help program. She alone helped dozens of Spanish-speaking students from nearby elementary and middle schools. The library also offered a number of programs and events geared toward African American patrons, and the majority of those who attended the story-time program were children from minority groups.

Experiences

After I was hired, I contacted Latino community leaders to build connections with the rapidly growing Spanish-speaking community in Southside Richmond. Those leaders included the manager of the Office of Multicultural Affairs for the city of Richmond, Radio Poder (the Spanish-language radio station), the Virginia Hispanic Chamber of Commerce, teachers from the RPS-system English-as-a-second-language (ESL) program, and staff from area nonprofit organizations. Through these contacts, I was able to secure on-air interviews on several radio programs, two in Spanish and one in English. In addition, I was contacted by reporters from local newspapers that serve the Hispanic/Latino community to conduct interviews focused on promoting the hiring of Richmond's first bilingual Latina library manager. The goal of the interviews was to raise awareness about the services the library offered to the Latino community and to encourage Spanish speakers to apply for library cards regardless of their immigration status. The interview highlighted important services that would allow Spanish speakers to complete employment applications and homework, practice reading and English-language skills, and take advantage of such recreational resources as movie viewings and other programs.

Challenges

The marketing campaign and community-engagement strategies were successful, but they introduced a number of challenges the library had not anticipated. Soon Spanish-speaking and Latino families and community members began visiting the library to register for library cards and to use the services, increasing the gate count to more than 500 patrons per day. The homework-help program reached capacity, and for the first time, children had to wait for assistance. In addition, the staff did not have the necessary language skills to assist patrons who spoke languages other than English. Offering expanded services to the Spanish-speaking population required that library personnel gain additional language skills in order to effectively serve and create a welcoming environment for Spanish-speaking patrons.

As soon as I had an opportunity to hire a librarian, I requested permission from the city of Richmond to include "Spanish language preferred" as a criterion in the job description. All candidates who indicated Spanish-language skills on their job applications and résumés were asked questions in Spanish during the on-site interviews. The rationale for this strategy was to assist the hiring panel with selecting those applicants whose Spanish-language proficiency ranged from the intermediate to superior levels. Adding this criterion to the application and interview processes led to hiring a bilingual librarian. These same criteria were later used when the library hired a library assistant for one of its branches. Subsequently, an internal staff member who had a good working knowledge of Spanish and could assist other staff members was hired for the position.

Lessons Learned

I spent a total of four years strengthening the cultural, social, and linguistic capacity at the Broad Rock Library. Community engagement was an important goal for the library, so personnel were encouraged to increase their awareness of local businesses, restaurants and the cuisine they served, nonprofit organizations, and houses of worship. Though the African American and Hispanic/Latino communities were the largest served, there were many other smaller minority constituencies representing religious, cultural, ethnic, and linguistic communities in Southside Richmond. Learning more about the various communities that the library serves allowed the staff to create programming targeted at those groups. To better meet the needs of the library's diverse patrons, the staff submitted purchase requests to the collection-management librarian to acquire additional resources. Our new programs and events were promoted to individuals who visited the Office of Multicultural Affairs (OMA) and via OMA's social media networks and radio broadcasts. By establishing relationships with OMA's clientele, the library was able to offer computer classes taught by Spanish-speaking volunteers. Other partnerships led to creating central Virginia's first and only Latino farmer's market, which was held weekly at the library. Library personnel were also encouraged to incorporate more culturally relevant programming, materials, and seasonal displays targeted to the African American community. This was achieved by bringing in presenters and speakers offering programs and music for the community.

I was confident that many of the diversity and inclusion programs that I had created during my tenure at RPL would be sustainable when I departed for a new position with Henrico County Public Library (HCPL). RPL hired two staff members who spoke Spanish and had the cultural competence to continue creating programs and resources to serve the minority communities on Richmond's Southside. The culture of creating shared expectations and goals has continued, and in fact, the library now offers an Art Mondays program for school-age kids to create West African Adinkra prints, a bilingual homework-help/reading buddies program, and general education diploma (GED) classes.

SUBURBAN LIBRARY

In 2016, I accepted a position managing the Sandston Branch Library of the Henrico County Public Library System. Established in 1963 in central Virginia, HCPL has a service area population of more than 329,000 residents and has grown to include nine libraries. The system also offers a law library housed within the Tuckahoe Area Library and mobile services via its bookmobile. Henrico County demographics continue to change. Spanish is the most spoken language in the county after English, and the Henrico County Public Schools (HCPS) have more than 80 languages represented. There are large south-central Asian, southeast Asian, and eastern European communities (TownCharts.com, 2018). Members of some of these communities use the libraries that are closest to where they live. There are several other fast-growing minority communities that do not use the library services nearly as much as members of the African American and Hispanic/Latino communities. This is likely due to a number of factors, including lack of awareness of the resources available and not having libraries in their native countries.

Experiences

I joined the HCPL staff with a solid reputation for creating diverse and inclusive programs targeting multiple minority communities and, in particular, the Latino/Hispanic community. My initial months on the job were spent doing an environmental scan to gain an understanding of the strategies the library was already using to offer diverse and inclusive resources to the communities it serves. I was quickly offered the opportunity to chair the multicultural committee, whose membership was comprised of library personnel from headquarters and all locations. Leading the multicultural committee positioned me to gain a deep understanding of the programs, workshops, and resources available system-wide. In this new role, I assumed leadership for shaping diversity initiatives for the entire library system, including the bookmobile services. The monthly committee meetings provided an excellent opportunity for me to learn about the communities each library served, as well as successful diversity and inclusion programs that had been offered in the past. As a result, I was able to leverage the community connections that I had established during my years working for RPL and HCPL.

Through this network, I established a partnership with the Latin Ballet of Virginia to create a signature Hispanic Heritage Month performance. Black

History Month received new attention, and the multicultural committee focused on creating programming, events, and displays at every library location. The month of programs for Black History Month began with featuring
an up-and-coming Black microhistorian. This event led to her first collaboration with Henrico County.

Challenges

One of the challenges I encountered was being able to conduct outreach to a
large number of community members and not leave the library understaffed.
An incredibly successful solution came when I was offered a regular monthly
spot on *Enfoque a la Comunindad*, a Spanish-language weekly radio broad-
cast, with representatives from Chesterfield County, the city of Richmond,
and the city of Petersburg. Originally, the program did not have a regular
Henrico County representative, so I submitted a proposal to library administration to become that representative, and after a period of time, my request
was granted. Today, I join the radio program via my office phone, and for an
hour on the first Monday of the month, I promote HCPL programs and events
in Spanish.

Lessons Learned

I have learned through my experiences at HCPL that creating partnerships
with the staff across the system has been key to creating system-wide diversity and inclusive programming, events, and opportunities for the patrons.
Leveraging my existing network and learning to work effectively while keeping long-term goals in mind have proven invaluable at HCPL.

Working with staff and managers from each area and branch library has
allowed me to more effectively partner with community organizations.
Working together we leverage social media, newspaper articles, interviews,
and in-house posters and advertisements to promote our diverse programming. I have also begun to build a culture of diversity and inclusion in my
branch with displays, programs, and events. One of the staff members regularly creates lively displays to showcase different heritage months, and the
children's librarian has produced a program for Día de los libros (World
Book Day) to reach out to our Latino families in eastern Henrico.

LEADING AS A DIVERSITY LEADER

My experiences in urban and suburban public library settings have taught me
that you can lead a diverse and inclusive public library at any level and from
any background. While it is certainly helpful to have language skills or cross-
cultural competency, one does not necessarily need these skills to survey the

library and the community that surrounds it, study the demographics, begin to conduct outreach, and create a culture of diversity and inclusion. Once you understand the community or communities you serve, you can begin to start building relationships necessary to create community partners, conduct outreach, and develop programs to better reflect your patrons. You may also begin to envision how you can hire staff with diverse competencies, such as language or cultural skills, and even create a cadre of diverse volunteers to assist with programming and large events. Mehra and Davis (2015) identify a list of categories to consider when evaluating your libraries' responsiveness to diverse communities:

a. Abilities or (dis)abilities: People identified based on their learning abilities, socialization skills and other related or health defined characteristics such as special needs, physical or visual impairment, children with autism, etc.
b. Age: Populations distinguished according to age such as toddlers, children, young adults, tweens, teenagers, adults, elderly, etc.
c. Educational differences: Individual/groups identified based on their formal and/or informal educational levels of attainment that may include elementary, middle or high schooled, home-schooled, undergraduate students, graduate students, adult learners, etc.
d. Gender concerns: Individuals/groups distinguished by their biological sex and/or gender such as females, males, etc.
e. International: People from different national origins, residencies, or citizenship such as Chinese, Finnish, New Zealanders, etc.
f. LGBTQ: Lesbian, gay, bisexual, transgender, or queer individuals.
g. Local/regional: A focus on the needs of people of local, regional, and other geographic distributions in relation to a sense of place perceived by users related to the location of the agency in the minds and hearts of the user.
h. Racial/ethnic categories: Individuals/groups based on racial and/or ethnic backgrounds such as African American, Asian American, Caucasian, etc.
i. Religion: People of different religious backgrounds and/or spiritualities such as Christians, Hindus, Muslims, etc. (pp. 19–20)

My experiences at Broad Rock Library were formative and instrumental in my development as a manager. I was able to come into a newly renovated library and break ground through the creation of alliances with the diverse communities, serving as a trailblazer in initiating relationships and networks that were not previously there. The library staff understood the value of creating a culture of diversity and inclusion as better serving the Spanish-speaking and African American communities. Fortunately, I was also able to hire two staff members who could continue and expand on the work started under my tenure.

These positive experiences were accompanied with some challenges. To better support other initiatives, the library system could have benefited from additional resources, including more bilingual teachers, staff members, and print and electronic resources. Integrating the work undertaken at one branch library would have had more of an impact if there had been more system-wide collaboration and partnerships. From these experiences I learned to harness the power of relationships and the value of networking with community power brokers and Latino leaders. Leveraging the skills and resources of the staff was incredibly important in a system that had fewer staff members. Hiring is critical in this equation, and in order to implement your diversity and inclusion vision, one must stress the importance of hiring staff members who have the needed skill sets. Finally, you can build steps into your "diversity" plan so that your vision can grow and the library can evolve to meet ever-changing needs. For example, keeping up with demographic changes in nearby schools can give you an idea of the patrons you will be serving in future years.

From my time at the Sandston Branch Library, I absorbed very powerful lessons and experiences that have helped me as a diversity leader. Again, I was the first bilingual Latina library manager, and I broke ground when I was able to become chair of the multicultural committee. Through this role, I learned to build programs at multiple locations and coordinate system-wide programming with multimanager buy-in. Step building is important, as well, and in building a set of actionable and concrete goals and deliverables, I learned how to be patient. Having a number of early wins in securing exciting and groundbreaking programming helps build your case for ongoing exploration of new programs.

Becoming the *go-to diversity expert* in the library system brought an opportunity to partner with the Spanish-language radio station to offer a monthly program promoting events at the libraries. Each of the nine libraries serve very different communities that have different needs, but through a network of experience and expertise, they will continue to learn how to better serve their communities by creating customized programs, outreach experiences, and enhanced collections.

Regardless of your position, title, or background, you can be committed to creating a diverse and inclusive library. You can help lead changes that can affect other staff members and the organizational culture and benefit your diverse community members. Several components make up a diversity leader. The ability to set goals and establish a diversity vision for the staff, coworkers, and the library is a key component. It is also important to be able to communicate your values for change. If you lead with values, you can get more buy-in from those you work with, as well as influential or key community members you want to bring into your network. Finally, create opportunities for the staff to gain technical knowledge and professional development. There are many webinars, courses, and resources available online, in person, and through organizations that teach cultural competency, diversity training, and language skills. Explore the resources that your organization or your local government may offer, and extend those opportunities to staff.

REFERENCES

Chesterfield County Planning Department. (2010). 2010 community indicators report. County of Chesterfield, VA. Retrieved from http://www.chesterfield.gov/content2.aspx?id=3436

City-Data.com. (2017). Broad Rock neighborhood in Richmond, Virginia. Retrieved September 3, 2018, from http://www.city-data.com/neighborhood/Broad-Rock-Richmond-VA.html

Davis, D. M., & Hall, T. D. (2007). *Diversity counts.* American Library Association, Office for Research and Statistics, Office for Diversity. Retrieved from http://www.ala.org/aboutala/ sites/ala.org.aboutala/files/content/diversity/diversitycounts/diversitycounts_rev0.pdf

Mehra, B., & Davis, R. (2015). A strategic diversity manifesto for public libraries in the 21st century. *New Library World, 116*(1/2), 15–36.

Office of Management and Budget of the County of Henrico. (2016). Fiscal year 2017–2018 approved budget. County of Henrico, Laurel, VA. Retrieved from https://henrico.us/assets/ ApprovedBudgetFY18.pdf

TownCharts.com. (2018). Henrico County, VA. Retrieved September 3, 2018, from http:// www.towncharts.com/Virginia/Demographics/Henrico-County-VA-Demographics-data.html

Winston, M., & Li, H. (2007). Leadership diversity: A study of urban public libraries. *Library Quarterly: Information, Community, Policy, 77*(1), 61–82. Retrieved from https://doi.org/ 10.1086/512956

Yoshinaga, K. (2016, July 1). Babies of color are now the majority, census says. Retrieved September 3, 2018, from https://www.npr.org/sections/ed/2016/07/01/ 484325664/babies-of-color-are-now-the-majority-census-says

Chapter Seven

Aligning the Library's Strategy With the Parent Organization

Jerry Perry, Jennifer Nichols, Cheryl Neal,
Shawna Thompson, and Ping Situ

The master's tools will never dismantle the master's house

—Audre Lorde

Through the course of this chapter, which focuses on the alignment of library strategy for advancing diversity and inclusion work with the intentions of the library's parent organization, we ask the reader to consider a well-known quote from feminist scholar, activist, and poet Audre Lorde: "The master's tools will never dismantle the master's house" (Lorde, 1984, p. 110).

When we do the work of diversity and inclusion, we inevitably become involved in a critique of historically informed and supported means of exclusion that have led to systematic oppression and discrimination. When we apply that criticism to the institutions in which we work, we are engaging in risk-taking behaviors because our change agency challenges systems that unavoidably reward some and exclude others, and we are doing so within the context of our own home, the parent institution.

In this framing, the work of diversity and inclusion requires this risk. Healthy organizations acknowledge, support, and reward such engagement, knowing it is the right thing to do as a matter of consciousness and mission. Such risk taking is rewarded and recognized by our professional associations, in their own strategic plans, mission, and value statements. Critical theory as it informs professional practice is also in ascendency, to judge by the discourse in the librarianship community of practice ignited by challenges to the long-held notion of library neutrality (Bourg, 2015; de jesus, 2014) and the role of libraries in response to violent, militarized policing approaches, especially in communities of color (Pagowsky & Wallace, 2015).

On a local level, critically informed approaches to the performance of work are also in ascendency. At the University of Arizona Libraries (UAL), in our Research and Learning Department, a critical approach to how we conduct information literacy instruction is an important aspect of how we frame our liaison-based instructional work, which led us to sponsor a transformational Critical Librarianship and Pedagogy Symposium in 2015, with a second held in November 2018.

In order to appreciate our approach, it is important to establish the context of the University of Arizona (UA) in our state. UA was established in 1885 and was the first university in what was then the Arizona Territory. With more than 44,000 students as of 2017, it is a major employer in the city of Tucson and a Carnegie Foundation RU/VH-level public research university with a land-grant mission.

The access mission of a land-grant university defines our charge to the state in the context of our setting and establishes the expectations of achievement to which we strive with a focus on the practical sciences, such as agriculture, engineering, and the sciences. Our access mission necessarily includes diverse communities because where we live in southern Arizona is diverse. Our region of southern Arizona was part of Mexico as recently as 1853, when lands south of the Gila River and west of the Rio Grande were purchased by the U.S. government from Mexico, known as the Gadsden Purchase/Venta de la Mesilla. Our connections to Mexico and Mexican culture remain strong; UA has recently become a Hispanic-serving institution in part to recognize these historically deep community connections and traditions. Prior to the arrival of Hispanic migrants and settlers, our region was home for millennia to indigenous communities, primarily but not exclusively the Tohono O'odham people and their ancestors.

As of 2016, according to the Making Action Possible for Southern Arizona (MAP) Dashboard Project, a multipartner initiative including the Community Foundation of Southern Arizona, the Pima Association of Governments, the Southern Arizona Leadership Council, and the University of Arizona, more than 36% of Tucson's residents were Hispanic, nearly twice the U.S. average. Tucson ranked last out of 12 western metropolitan statistical areas (MSA) for population growth, with a 2015–2016 rate of growth of only 0.4%. Tucson places in the bottom third when compared with other regions in the western United States for median wages ($33,970) and labor force participation rates (just under 80% for ages 25 to 54). In sum, ours is an ethnically diverse and economically challenged community.

At UAL we have embraced the risk that comes with approaching our work critically, in interrogating the master's house. We do this with the knowledge that our parent institution has embraced a model of diversity and inclusion, known as Inclusive Excellence, that anticipates critical appraisal and recognizes historical and contemporary challenges for residents in the community. According to the Association of American Colleges and Universities (AACU), Inclusive Excellence "is designed to help colleges and universities integrate diversity, equity, and educational quality efforts into their missions and institutional operations" (n.d., para. 1). In this chapter, we introduce the model of Inclusive Excellence as a framework for encouraging and integrating sustainable diversity and inclusion work in service to the mission of the academy and, in our instance at UA, in alignment with our parent organization's most pressing priorities. We offer our efforts to align our work as an example, involving the interrogation and critique of our master using the tools of Inclusive Excellence and illustrated through a case-study approach. We demonstrate how we have critically engaged with this model, allowing us to assess our own assets and deficiencies (critical appraisal) and map our findings to the model's broader institutional framework, prioritized by our parent institution.

By engaging with the institutionally sanctioned Inclusive Excellence model, we have intentionally aligned our efforts around diversity and inclusion with the priorities of our parent organization. In so doing, we are using the master's tools to "dismantle" systems of exclusion in our own house (both our library and our parent institution) through critical appraisal, as well as introducing new tools to build a stronger home for all.

As we consider the health and vitality of our parent institution, our efforts have also included intentional use of the house-building tool of self-care. We have done so through transformative acts, such as our contributions to a campus movement to address the demands of marginalized student communities, our critical approaches to informational literacy instruction, and our embracement of an inclusive and intentional cocreation model of engagement around our makerspace services.

We have also applied the tool of self-care to the library's work as we establish a living community of practice around diversity and inclusion. Our primary accomplishment of self-care was the creation of a Diversity, Social Justice and Equity Council (DSJEC). This chapter addresses the formation and work of this community of practice within our university home and describes how the council has supported a learning culture around diversity and inclusion through programming, teaching, and learning opportunities in our library.

THE UNIVERSITY OF ARIZONA LIBRARIES

From a modest beginning as a mining college in the late 1880s, UA now annually receives in excess of $600 million in research funding. According to the 2015–2016 Association of Research Libraries' "Spending by University Research Libraries" report, UA libraries are ranked 37th overall for university investment. The libraries are made up of 8 departments with nearly 200 employees. UAL promotes five core values that employees strive to incorporate into their work, including diversity, continuous learning, innovation, collaboration, and integrity (UAL, n.d.b). By way of the diversity value, "We enrich our work through the exchange of many voices and ideas" (UAL, n.d.b, para. 1).

As articulated in its mission statement, UAL explicitly aligns itself in service to the broader university's strategic vision: "The University of Arizona Libraries are enterprising partners in advancing the University's priorities. We cultivate an environment that promotes inquiry, creative endeavor, scholarly communication and lifelong learning. Our resources, services and expertise enrich the lives of Arizonans, and contribute to an expanding global academic community" (UAL, n.d.a, para. 2). UAL's vision posits the libraries as "the intellectual crossroads of the University, enabling innovative interdisciplinary research, scholarship and creative endeavor" (UAL, n.d.a, para. 3). The libraries strategic plan "outlines how we are advancing the University strategic priorities of student engagement, research innovation, community partnership and synergy."

BUILDING A BETTER HOME FOR ALL: INCLUSIVE EXCELLENCE

The UA's Office for Diversity and Inclusive Excellence (ODIEX) defines the idea of Inclusive Excellence as "the systemic, institutional, cultural transformation approach to campus diversity—[it] is designed to engage the rich array of students, staff, faculty, administrators, and alumni in the work of embedding diversity and inclusiveness throughout the University of Arizona. The goal is to create an engaged university that creates a welcoming campus climate that capitalizes on diversity" (ODIEX, n.d., para. 1).

UA has evolved over the years from a university that recognizes the value and importance of diversity to an institution that also acknowledges the need to address diversity and inclusion in a systemic way. Contextually, it is important to remember incidents that have had a national impact. In November 2015, students at the University of Missouri announced a list of demands after months of racial incidents and calls for the university administration to address their concerns (Izadi, 2015). These actions sparked a movement across institutions of higher education in North America, with the University of Arizona being no exception. In March 2016, the list of demands was released after a listening tour by then–UA president Ann Weaver Hart, in which student leaders felt there was not sufficient action in response to their frustrations and where two protests "marked a 'tipping point' for various campus cultural organizations that represent the UA's marginalized students" (Jacquette, 2016). President Hart then convened a diversity task force to address these needs, and Associate Dean of Libraries Jerry Perry served as a representative faculty administrator (Gross, 2016). Students were asking for campus leaders to build them a better home, and though there were numerous blueprints, there was no one contracted to do the work.

Simultaneously, the provost's Diversity Coordinating Council began planning for the creation of an office for diversity and the hiring of a senior diversity officer. After a nationwide search, UA hired a diversity officer to lead the ODIEX, established in August 2016. ODIEX serves as the hub and champion, providing guidance to 24 diversity committees across the institution. Deans and senior administrators were asked to create committees in each academic college and administrative unit. Comprised of faculty, staff, and students from each college, the committees were tasked with undertaking a review of current efforts and identifying areas for improvement in their units. To assist in the assessment, personnel from ODIEX created an implementation guidebook with which committees were charged to assess dimensions of their domains for areas and initiatives where diversity and inclusiveness had already been embedded and to identify institutional aspects lacking in diversity and inclusiveness. Examples of areas that were to be assessed included mission statements, goals and values, leadership, human resources, student advising and curriculum, faculty promotion and tenure, and so forth.

DSJEC AND THE INCLUSIVE EXCELLENCE GUIDEBOOK: A CASE STUDY

In the fall of 2016, each campus unit was asked by Dr. Jesus Treviño, incoming director of the Office of Diversity and Inclusive Excellence, to complete the ODIEX guidebook, *Transforming the UA Into an Inclusive Excellence University for the 21st Century: A Guidebook for Implementing and Practicing Inclusive Excellence.* This multipage document included an inventory, an analysis, an action plan, and an assessment.

As a newly appointed council of the library's administration, DSJEC experienced internal conflict as we established our authority and tested our commitment to diversity and inclusion. After the first year of commitment and investment, we created a vibrant, dedicated council that stands ready to continue the work of diversity and inclusion for UAL.

The inventory period highlighted DSJEC's confusion about our authority. "Who were we to inventory the whole UAL as just a group of twelve?" asked some who found the task monumental. Others stated, "If not us, then who?" As we came to terms with our right to represent the work, we compiled raw comments that we considered to be honest and useful. The inventory consisted of 28 sections with multiple questions. For example, the leadership section consisted of four questions:

- Do *top-level* unit administrators express the value of diversity and inclusiveness at speaking engagements?
- Have *top-level* administrators participated in diversity and inclusiveness training?
- Have leaders allocated resources to support diversity and inclusiveness initiatives?
- Does the unit have a diversity and inclusiveness plan?

DSJEC recommended to library leadership that the inventory responses be considered a snapshot in time and a document that defined our future work. After meeting our deadline for the inventory, we began working on the summary analysis and action plan, including a marked-up inventory highlighting UAL's areas of strength, as well as areas where more information was needed and those needing improvement. A high/low chart was created of what could be easily done versus what would take significantly more effort to do. Most of the conversation in DSJEC meetings focused on how to incorporate a diversity question into our annual performance evaluations. Confidentiality was essential as we discussed personal views, as well as campus-wide and national events and initiatives.

Through the summer, DSJEC met with Treviño and reported our progress on the guidebook. We presented at a libraries' all-staff meeting and informed our colleagues about our work in a presentation entitled "Transforming the University of Arizona Into an Inclusive Excellence University for the 21st Century: A Guidebook for Implementing and Practicing Inclusive Excellence; or, What the Heck Has the Diversity, Social Justice and Equity Council (DSJEC) Been Up To?" During this period, the DSJEC struggled to stay purposeful in both creating programming and completing the ODIEX analysis. Our distraction mirrored challenges in the broader culture. The creation of DSJEC coincided with these broader challenges. From our inception, we dealt with fear for our UA Deferred Action for Childhood Arrivals (DACA) students due to the Donald Trump campaign and presidency, including proposed immigration policies and travel bans potentially affecting our campus. Letters of interest to participate in DSJEC were written in the aftermath of the Pulse nightclub massacre in July 2016. In November, Donald Trump was elected president, and in December the libraries participated with Tucson's One Community March and Vigil of Affirmation. The Women's March was held in January 2017, the day after the inauguration, followed by a travel ban affecting people worldwide, and UA affiliates were no exception. Charlottesville and the University of Virginia was the site of a White nationalist rally in August 2017, including a man driving a car into the crowd protesting the rally and resulting in the death of a woman. During the 2017 hurricane season, Harry, Irma, and Maria tore through Texas, Puerto Rico, Haiti, the Dominican Republic, and the U.S. Virgin Islands.

Throughout these controversies and disasters, DSJEC asked, "How do we respond?" and "How should administrators respond?" Members grappled with establishing a shared understanding of what appropriate responses administration should convey. Some members interpreted a lack of public statements as a failure to address fears, concerns, and needs of support, sensing a lack of compassion or empathy for adverse events that seemingly did not directly affect UAL. Despite these difficulties, DSJEC continues to better align our organization's vision and voice with the goals of ODIEX.

Since its inception, DSJEC has met at minimum every two weeks. For many members it is a safe place to discuss, vent, and regroup. One member commented, "If I didn't have DSJEC, I wouldn't be here or able to function with all the controversies, traumas, and worldwide events that impact all of us." We recently compiled a list of accomplishments for fiscal year 2017–2018. Much of this work included reenvisioning our purpose and clarifying the roles of the council's officers. We established member term lengths and a way to stagger memberships to avoid losing momentum. The DSJEC activities of 2017 enriched our lives, and feisty honesty during our DSJEC retreat brought new and charter members into alignment.

Most recently, the library has embarked on creating a new strategic map, using design-thinking methodologies to create a flexible and iterative plan for the next 18 months. As the library staff and the faculty strategized and listened to one another over a six-month period, they committed one of the four strategic directions to the organizational value of diversity, which is included in the following statement:

> We strive to be a champion of diversity, social justice, and equity in our own organization and in how we work with campus and community colleagues. We are committed to
>
> • creating for our users and ourselves welcoming, respectful, and inclusive spaces, services, and practices that meet diverse needs; and
> • promoting many viewpoints in the way we collect, manage, and share our distinctive collections for campus and community enrichment.

Our annual action plan is nearly complete, and we are excited to present our recommendations to leadership. *Is leadership ready to hear us?* We believe so, though it is not clear that we have successfully co-opted the master's tools. But in completing the inventory, assembling a strong council, and looking forward with the strategic map embracing diversity, social justice, and inclusion, we are ready to implement change.

CREATING OUR OWN TOOLS: SELF-CARE

Programming is hard. It is time-consuming, and the required labor is often unseen, unaccounted for, and gendered. In the first 18 months of the council's existence, one of the key areas of engagement with the library staff was through purposeful programming. In April 2017, the council hosted, with noted diversity trainer Dr. Brenda Allen, kickoff events that included sessions on implicit bias, inclusive leadership, and communicating differences. With nearly 40% of the staff taking part in the event, this kickoff was well attended and served as a signal to the organization that programming on diversity and inclusion was valuable and intended to provide tools for further self-improvement, as well as organizational growth. Other programming open to library staff included "Deconstructing Unconscious Bias Through Empathy," an allyship workshop, and a visit from peer institution University of Michigan Libraries.

This year, as the council has transitioned to its second iteration with three new members, we have taken a pause. For our group, self-care has encouraged us to define how we embark on meaningful programming without overburdening ourselves. How can we position ourselves to be responsive and to be ready to host opportunities when they indeed feel like opportunities rather than burdens? In this mind-set, we have provided access to a microaggressions webinar, with a facilitated follow-up conversation. While the council was initially disappointed in the small turnout, upon reflection, the opportunity to have a personal, intimate conversation with self-reflection was both worthwhile and celebrated. Additionally, the Arizona Library Association approached us to host a regional forum on diversity and inclusion for southern Arizona. Having the flexibility to be in partnership with diversity efforts without having to be the primary providers of content enables us to be responsive and bring additional programming to our staff and faculty without insurmountable burdens of extra caretaking. In other words, as one's counselor might encourage through self-care, we can achieve more meaningful and balanced opportunities that make sense for the organization and contribute to a healthy community.

CULTIVATING THE FRONT YARD

Meanwhile, the library's pilot makerspace, the iSpace, has grown, somewhat like an organic community garden. Progress was rapid and included many necessary partners, thus it was imperative for us to create a makerspace that was inclusive and a model of what a makerspace could be in this arena.

The librarians directing the growth of the iSpace intentionally focused on the cultivation of a community of makers. In such a large university, it was important that we create a space that felt open, accessible, and responsive to the needs of the community. Makerspaces are traditionally populated by young White males who self-identify as "techie" in some way (Faulkner & McClart, 2014). Contributing to this has been the rise of the *Make* magazine, under criticism from feminist scholars for the co-opting of the maker movement by this population and disregarding the long traditions of crafting and such traditionally feminized arts as sewing, embroidery, and so forth (Buechley, 2013; Justice & Markus, 2010). Therefore, the cultivation of an intentional community has been central to the efforts of the iSpace librarians, and the creation of high-profile events to foster this community has been integral to growing success. Annual events, such as the Women Techmaker's Hackathon and monthly WTF (Women, Trans, Femme) Maker Nights, exemplify the efforts.

CONCLUSION

The work of Inclusive Excellence is not quick and efficient work. As outlined here, our efforts to make significant changes to our master's house were met with the realities of the 21st-century academic institution—limited resources, competing campus priorities, and changing administrations, set in a broader cultural moment in our country rife with conflict. How should we in the academic library community of practice respond to and engage with real racial and ethnic tensions on our campuses and in our communities? How do we as library workers sustain our labor in light of deep and traumatic challenges to what we once thought of as shared core values? Creating a genuinely inclusive atmosphere in the UAL has not been an easy endeavor. Despite these challenges, UAL remains committed to do what we can to foster diversity and inclusion by making the library a welcoming place for everyone. DSJEC at the UAL is doing its best to be a leader in integrating inclusion, diversity, social justice, and equity into all aspects of the life of the library community, as well as the campus at large.

REFERENCES

Association of American Colleges and Universities (AACU). (n.d.). Making excellence inclusive. Retrieved from https://www.aacu.org/making-excellence-inclusive

Bourg, C. (2015, January 28). Never neutral: Libraries, technology, and inclusion. Retrieved from Feral Librarian (blog), https://chrisbourg.wordpress.com/2015/01/28/never-neutral-libraries-technology-and-inclusion/

Buechley, L. (2013). Thinking about making: Keynote. Retrieved from https://edstream.stanford.edu/Video/Play/883b61dd951d4d3f90abeec65eead2911d

de jesus, n. (2014, September 24). Locating the library in institutional oppression. Retrieved from http://www.inthelibrarywiththeleadpipe.org/2014/locating-the-library-in-institutional-oppression/

Faulkner, S., & McClart, A. (2014). Making change: Can ethnographic research about women makers change the future of computing? *Ethnographic Praxis in Industry Conference Proceedings* (pp. 187–198). Retrieved from https://doi: 10.1111/1559–8918.01026

Gross, S. (2016, March 20). Hart announces diversity task force. *Daily Wildcat*. Retrieved from http://www.wildcat.arizona.edu/article/2016/03/hart-announces-diversity-task-force-to-ad dress-campus-cultural-competency-and-diversity-issues

Izadi, E. (2015, November 9). The incidents that led to the University of Missouri president's resignation. *Washington Post*. Retrieved from https://www.washingtonpost.com/news/grade-point/wp/2015/11/09/the-incidents-that-led-to-the-university-of-missouri-presidents-resignation/?utm_term=.03aa22d75656

Jacquette, M. (2016, March 8). Protesters make demands for marginalized students. *Daily Wildcat*. Retrieved from http://archive.li/7ypJ8

Justice, S., & Markus, S. (2010). Educators, gender equity and making: Opportunities and obstacles. Retrieved from http://www.academia.edu/16570000/Educators_Gender_Equity _and_Making_Opportunities_and_Obstacles

Lorde, A. G. (1984). The master's tools will never dismantle the master's house. In *Sister outsider: Essays and speeches* (pp. 110–114). Trumansburg, NY: Crossing Press.

Making Action Possible for Southern Arizona. (2014). Workforce and demographics overview. Retrieved from https://mapazdashboard.arizona.edu/workforce-demographics-overview

Office for Diversity and Inclusive Excellence (ODIEX). (n.d.). About ODIEX. Retrieved from https://diversity.arizona.edu/odiex

Pagowsky, N., & Wallace, N. (2015). Black lives matter! Shedding library neutrality rhetoric for social justice. *College and Research Libraries News, 76*(4), 196–214. Retrieved from https://crln.acrl.org/index.php/crlnews/article/view/9293/10374

University of Arizona Libraries (UAL). (n.d.a). Our organization. Retrieved from http://new.library.arizona.edu/about/organization

University of Arizona Libraries (UAL). (n.d.b). Our values. Retrieved from http://new.library.arizona.edu/sites/default/files/ua-libraries-values.pdf

Chapter Eight

Recruiting and Retaining a Diverse Workforce

Shannon D. Jones and Beverly Murphy

The world needs different kinds of minds to work together.

—Dr. Temple Grandin

Increasing racial and ethnic diversity in librarianship has been a stated priority in librarianship for years. Professional associations, such as the American Library Association (ALA) and the Association of Research Libraries (ARL), have made strides toward this priority by creating programs to help recruit people of color into librarianship. Some of these programs have been successful at recruiting students of color into library and information science (LIS) programs, but the yield promised by these programs has not been realized. Language related to diversity and inclusion (D&I) has been included in strategic plans, but in many cases the plans have not been operationalized well. Throughout this book, authors discuss a variety of diversity and inclusion issues that affect the business of libraries and their workforces. This chapter, however, focuses exclusively on practical strategies and real-life considerations that must be taken into account when recruiting and retaining diverse individuals for library teams.

Three factors have emerged that make diversity recruitment and retention efforts in libraries essential: the demographic data from ALA revealing a lack of workforce diversity; the changing population demographics; and the current social, cultural, and political climate affecting our communities.

The American Library Association, the Association of College and Research Libraries (ACRL) and other associations have invested heavily in creating and sustaining programs designed to recruit individuals from traditionally underrepresented groups to the profession, yet the needle has moved very little. ALA's *Diversity Counts* study (conducted in 2006, released in 2007, and updated in 2012) is a comprehensive study of gender, race, and age in the library profession. The study provided a benchmark for the initiatives of the ALA, documenting the state of the profession before the launch of several diversity recruitment initiatives—most notably the Spectrum Scholarship Program begun in 1997. It also served as a call to action, demonstrating progress within the profession but confirming the continued need to invest time and resources into the recruitment of a more diverse workforce (American Library Association, 2012).

The *Diversity Counts* study surveyed 110,000 librarians at a wide range of institutions and found that 88% of respondents were White and 82% were women (American Library Association, 2012). The results showed that not only were individuals from diverse racial and ethnic background groups a small percentage of the workforce but also the numbers were significant in showing that the workforce in U.S. libraries did not reflect the communities being served. Although efforts to diversify librarianship have gradually improved, it continues to be a largely homogenous profession. We believe that, if this study were currently conducted, these same results would persist.

By contrast, the U.S. population has grown more diverse. Statistics from the U.S. Census Bureau show that the demographic makeup of communities is continuing to change, as shown in the following population data: 50.8% female, 13% persons 65 years and older, 13.2% foreign-born, 61.3% White, 13.3% Black or African American, 1.3% American Indian and Alaska Native, 5.7% Asian, 0.2% Native Hawaiian and other Pacific Islander, 17.8% Hispanic or Latino, and 2.6% two or more races (U.S. Census Bureau, 2016). These census numbers are critical to keep in mind when thinking about the future of libraries and the role they play in their respective communities. Instead of reflecting one group of the population, libraries should reflect the communities they serve.

It is also critical to pay attention to social, cultural, and political factors that are affecting communities across the United States because these larger movements may be hampering diversity and retention efforts. With the elections of the 44th and 45th presidents of the United States, some ugly and hurtful racial tensions have blatantly surfaced in our country. Historical moments that should have been celebrated have been overshadowed and short-lived as the U.S. public deals with the hard-core truth that racism, sexism, and homophobia are still alive and well. Countless news stories and social media postings demonstrate that individuals in cities across the country have deep-seated hostilities toward those with diverse ethnicities, gender identities, sexual orientations, physical abilities, and other backgrounds. This hostile environment is often heightened through social media.

It is not uncommon these days to see homophobic, sexist, or racist posts on Twitter or Facebook. Thanks to camera phones and Facebook Live, exposure to these types of interactions spread like a raging wildfire in a matter of minutes. The reality is that some of the same people who use social media as a platform to spread hate-filled messages bring these same attitudes and sentiments to the workplace and oftentimes are in positions to make hiring decisions. Your library must be prepared to deliver a cogent message making the case for your environment as a safe and welcoming place to work, since some people may not want to work in communities where members have been shown to be intolerant.

RECRUITMENT

There is an African proverb that says *it takes a village to raise a child*. The same is true when it comes to recruiting and retaining a diverse workforce. The library should take a holistic approach when developing its recruitment plan by involving personnel from a variety of functional roles and levels. Recruiting the right talent to the library is time-consuming and expensive but necessary to support existing and emerging initiatives. It can be one of the most rewarding and challenging tasks that a library undertakes. But it could become even more challenging when recruiting candidates from diverse backgrounds, whether the distinction is gender, race, ethnicity, age, sexual identity, or something else.

The overall goal of any recruitment plan is to attract the most qualified individuals to your team. The first step in developing this plan is to assess the library's environment and readiness for employing diverse individuals. So before any recruitment activities take place, libraries need to prepare their environments for diverse candidates. This preparation includes working with the staff on issues related to cultural competence, implicit bias, microaggressions, and conflict management. Another aspect of this preparation includes defining what *qualified* means to the library. This will require a discussion with the library's managers and an assessment of the skill sets needed to assist the library with meeting its mission.

One of the best strategies for preparing the library's environment includes an assessment of the library's personnel, collections, and programs. Key questions to ask include the following:

- Does the library's personnel reflect the communities it serves?
- Have library personnel been prepared to work with patrons and colleagues from diverse backgrounds?
- Does the library offer staff-development opportunities that promote diverse and inclusive programs?
- Has a concerted effort been made to inform and educate library personnel about diversity and inclusion issues?

- Does the library provide a welcoming, safe, and inclusive environment?
- Does the library space meet the needs of diverse patrons?
- How does library programing and services meet the needs of all patrons, regardless of age, ethnicity, race, religion, sexual orientation, political view, or socioeconomic status?

The answers to these questions will provide insight into whether diversity issues are actively being addressed or if the library has more work to do. One of the most visible indicators of whether a library is diverse is looking at the racial and ethnic demographic of the staff as compared to that of the community served. Keep in mind that most candidates visit the library's website (including the employee directory) when preparing their application or for the interview, if selected. After reviewing information, including pictures of the staff posted to the library's website, a candidate from an underrepresented group may ponder the following:

- Are there others of my ethnicity employed by the library?
- If not, should I reevaluate my interest if I'm the only one?
- Will I fit in?
- Will I even get a chance to interview?

Giving thought to these candidate-centered questions allows library personnel to view the application and interview processes from the candidate's perspective.

The second strategy in the preparation process is to think about the knowledge and skill sets needed by the workforce to support current campus initiatives while considering the information-seeking behaviors and traits of the audiences served. Libraries and the constituents they serve are vastly different than they were 20 years ago. These differences have required that the library workforce move beyond the traditional, assume different roles, participate in newfound work, and try novel approaches to getting the work done. The types of individuals recruited, the skills required, and the process used to attract personnel has also changed. Many of today's libraries have big, bold, and far-reaching organizational visions that align with the university's strategy to expand diversity and inclusion. Supporting these ambitious visions requires the library to employ personnel who have the knowledge and skills to act on the library's vision.

The third strategy is to develop a strategic plan that includes a clear vision for diversity and inclusion. Librarians have the opportunity to take a leadership role in making it clear that diversity and inclusion is a key element of the library's strategic plan and an important aspect of recruitment. Having diversity and inclusion language written into the strategic plan listing specific, actionable, and measurable goals will allow libraries to demonstrate a clear commitment to this work. The final D&I plan should be posted on the library's website for potential candidates to review. Once diversity and inclusion goals are established, library staff must make a true commitment to ensure that the goals become a reality by not only giving their buy-in but also demonstrating belief in their actions.

The fourth strategy in the preparation process is to assess the library's organizational climate. One strategy that libraries have used to uncover staff attitudes about diversity and inclusion is administering a climate survey, such as ARL's ClimateQUAL. ClimateQUAL "is an assessment of library staff perceptions concerning (a) their library's commitment to the principles of diversity, (b) organizational policies and procedures, and (c) staff attitudes. It is an online survey with questions designed to understand the impact perceptions have on service quality in a library setting" (Association of Research Libraries, n.d.a). It is not a survey about quality itself but rather a survey of staff attitudes that shape the culture of the organization and have led to the development of a new concept that we call the "healthy organization" (Lowry, 2011, p. 221). Lowry notes that "a healthy organization has policies, practices, and procedures that empower employees and emphasize the importance of continual learning and innovation to meet the demands of an ever changing environment" (Lowry & Hanges, 2008, p. 3). He goes on to say that a healthy organization is one where customer service, employee diversity, and organizational justice are all recognized as critical imperatives that will determine the effectiveness of the organization in the long run (Lowry & Hanges, 2008, p. 3). The ultimate benefit of administering a climate survey is that it allows the library administration to assess its readiness for maintaining and supporting an environment that is safe, inclusive, and welcoming. This information will be helpful as the library recruits people from various backgrounds.

The fifth strategy in preparing the library to recruit people from underrepresented groups is identifying the people who will serve on the search committee. The primary responsibility of the search committee is to recruit, to screen, and to recommend the best candidates for a given position. It's extremely important that search committee members are carefully selected because of the significant role it plays in whether people from underrepresented groups make the cut. A well-constructed search committee should include a diverse group of people to ensure that a range of opinions is represented. This will also bring balance to the search committee since we all have unconscious biases that may hinder our ability to select the best candidates. Individuals who do not see the need for diversity or its benefit should not serve on search committees. We are convinced that one of the reasons a number of qualified applicants do not get interviews is because of the personal biases of individual search committee members. These biases, judgments, and micro-aggressions manifest in the language used when talking about applicants.

People tend to want to hire people who are just like them, so they use themselves as a "proxy to judge is that person going to be good on the job?" (Elmer, 2012). This creates issues because even those of us who believe we are fair and inclusive act on implicit biases that influence our decisions despite our best efforts. Implicit biases contribute to applicants being pre-judged and underestimated. "We have a bias when, rather than being neutral, we have a preference for (or aversion to) a person or group of people. Thus, we use the term 'implicit bias' to describe when we have attitudes towards people or associate stereotypes with them without our conscious knowledge" (Perception Institute, n.d.). For instance, we've served on a number of search committees where one or both of us have heard some of the following state-ments:

- I don't know if the person will fit in here because he or she works at a historically Black college and university (HBCU).
- I'm not sure if the candidate will be able to make the transition to our library because he or she works at a smaller institution or at a public library.
- I don't know if I want to work for him, but I'd like to go have a beer with him.
- I'm just not sure if the person is a good fit.

Because of the implicit biases these statements reflect, some candidates are not assessed on the experiences or skills they would bring to the job but often are judged based on people's personal opinions and preconceived notions rather than established evaluation criteria. Elmer writes, "A majority of the hiring managers ranked cultural fit—the similarity to existing employees' backgrounds, hobbies, and presentation—as the most important criterion dur-ing a job interview" (2012). Helping people to acknowledge that they have implicit biases can be accomplished by providing training and development on the topic.

Finally, the sixth strategy is to prepare individuals to work as part of a diverse staff once new employees are recruited; many libraries offer profes-sional development and training opportunities to learn new skills. Training in diversity and inclusion, cultural competence, implicit bias, and microaggres-sions is essential for everyone who works in a library. Diversity creates an interesting environment, making us smarter and oftentimes forcing us to consider ideas and concepts that we would not have if the environment were homogenous. As African American women, we can clearly see the world through that lens, but it is our responsibility to make a conscious effort to see the world from another's point of view. It is also our responsibility to ac-knowledge that unconscious biases are at work in every encounter and that we must work to overcome them. The first step in overcoming implicit bias is to take Harvard's Implicit Association Test (IAT), which measures attitudes and beliefs that people may be unwilling or unable to report (Project Implicit, 2011).

Getting to Know Your Community

It is often helpful to applicants from underrepresented groups if the library staff is familiar with the resources available on campus and within the local community. For instance, identifying faculty and staff members from underrepresented groups might be useful as a support system. These individuals could be invited to participate in the recruitment process by serving on the search committee, having lunch or dinner with the candidate, or attending the candidate's interview presentation. These strategies will allow the applicant to see that there are other diverse personnel on campus with whom he or she could network. Having an awareness of campus-based resources, such as the location of designated safe zones or gender-neutral restrooms, will go a long way toward helping potential employees feel welcome and included in your library. Another helpful strategy would be to create a handout for potential recruits that list such resources as realtors, restaurants, beauty salons, barber shops, places of worship, cultural events, and activities. This type of document would make a nice addition to a folder of materials prepared for the interviewee. Examples of community resources that may offer applicants insight into the local community include such organizations as the Hispanic Chamber of Commerce or publications like the Black Pages directory. These types of resources will be helpful as potential employees consider relocation and whether your library or the city in which it operates is right for them, as well as the possibilities for maintaining a lifestyle outside of work.

Strengthening the Pipeline

Increasing the pipeline of diverse individuals to assume positions in libraries requires creative strategies. Several libraries have found establishing residency programs to be a successful recruitment strategy for hiring personnel from underrepresented groups. The results from a 2017 survey conducted by ARL identified several approaches that member libraries have found helpful, including training search committee members on how to develop a diverse candidate pool; sending job ads to participants of diversity enhancement recruitment programs, such as ARL's Initiative to Recruit a Diverse Workforce (IRDW) and ALA's Spectrum Scholars; offering a post-LIS residency program; and supporting ARL initiatives that attract librarians from racially and ethnically diverse groups to the profession.

Despite best efforts, there will be barriers to recruiting a diverse applicant pool that will likely be beyond the library's control. A majority of those responding to the ARL survey (37% or 63%) identified real and perceived barriers to recruitment. The most common barriers continue to be related to the library's geographic location and the reputation of the city, state, or university as not welcoming diverse individuals. Others mentioned the small pools of diverse candidates in LIS programs and implicit bias of search committees or managers (Anaya & Maxey-Harris, 2017).

RETENTION

Max De Pree eloquently expresses our shared perspective on the importance of diversity and inclusion: "We need to give each other the space to grow, to be ourselves, to exercise our diversity. We need to give each other space so that we may both give and receive such beautiful things as ideas, openness, dignity, joy, healing, and inclusion" (De Pree, 1987, p. 17). Cultivating this type of environment where all members of the library team feel comfortable enough to share their most authentic selves is no easy task, and it will not happen overnight. In the previous section, we discuss the need for having a recruitment plan, and the same type of plan is needed for retaining employees from underrepresented groups.

In a 2007 white paper, Neely and Peterson list several recommendations that libraries should consider when working to retain minority employees, including offering orientations and welcomes; programming that addresses work culture issues, presented in a nonthreatening way, such as a social activity; opportunities for professional development; a positive environment that honors employee values, opinions, and voices; compensation and rewards; good management; and recognition of work-life balance needs (Neely & Peterson, 2007). Neely and Peterson also assert that, "while these activities would be useful for retaining all hires, they are especially significant for the retention of minority hires because they often do not have the same built-in communities/support systems that majority hires do" (2007, p. 7). Respondents to ARL's diversity and inclusion survey noted that the most commonly used retention strategies are onboarding/orientation programs for new staff, leadership development and training, mentoring programs to help librarians attain advancement and tenure, and supporting membership in or engagement with parent institution diversity affinity groups or ALA ethnic caucuses (Anaya & Maxey-Harris, 2017). Other strategies identified included the development of writing groups for all faculty members, travel funds for all library personnel, personal involvement and advocacy by library leadership, and library administrators who actively work to ensure a positive work culture (Anaya & Maxey-Harris, 2017, p. 6).

All retention activities should begin with the end in mind. Framing the retention process in this manner encourages the hiring manager to give some thought to how a librarian or paraprofessional will look once they leave the library or institution, whether it's 2 or 25 years later. Essentially the question is, *What effect will working in my library for any given time have on an individual psychologically, physiologically, and emotionally?* Assisting staff members with becoming the best versions of themselves should be a goal of all managers. Accomplishing this requires an encouraging and supportive environment that is thriving, safe, inclusive, and welcoming and one that inspires positive professional growth and allows staff members to bring their most authentic selves to work. For all intents and purposes, the library should be a place where patrons and staff alike can do their best work. Diverse personnel leave institutions for a variety of reasons, so libraries that don't offer this type of environment will find it hard to keep them on staff. The ARL survey showed that librarians left institutions because of limited advancement options, the lack of connection with staff, the culture of the university, and the lack of diversity in the local community (Anaya & Maxey-Harris, 2017, p. 5). Creating an environment where personnel from diverse backgrounds want to stay with the library requires the collective effort of all library personnel, but it begins at the top with the library's leadership.

Leaders bear the responsibility of keeping the mission of improving diversity and inclusion in mind during all recruitment efforts. Failure to do so can discourage staff members and make them less invested in the mission. For example, one of us attended a talk where the featured speaker responded that he did not think about diversity at all when asked about his thoughts on the role that diversity played in his unit. It was alarming to hear this statement from an individual who holds a senior-level position at the university and leads a unit that treats and cares for patients from diverse racial and ethnic backgrounds. It was equally disappointing to hear this because the university debuted an ambitious diversity and inclusion strategic plan in 2016. This plan resulted in the creation of the university's first-ever chief diversity officer, incorporating diversity and inclusion as one of the five themes in the university's strategic plan, four hours of mandatory diversity and inclusion training for all university employees, and a mandate that diversity and inclusion goals be included in all unit-level strategic plans. The plan was a huge undertaking but long overdue for a university that historically had a strained relationship with individuals from minority racial and ethnic backgrounds, especially as it related to hiring practices. As an individual from a traditionally underrepresented group, this plan is a source of excitement and frustration. It's exciting that the university has declared diversity as the right thing to do, but now based on this senior leader's comments, it's frustrating and worrisome that it's just lip service.

In an environment where the racial and ethnic makeup of the United States continues to change, we need more than just lip service from leaders. Diversity is essential to an organization's success and helping to meet varying needs of individuals from these groups. Meeting those needs requires that the organization pay attention to the unique cultural and societal issues that these groups deal with. Having an understanding of the expectations and needs of a transgendered paraprofessional, an African American or Latino librarian, or the employee with a mobility disability will likely go a long way toward ensuring that these employees feel safe, valued, respected, and productive at work.

Building Resilience

Another retention strategy is to encourage diverse personnel to build resilience. Dictionary.com defines *resilience* as the "ability to recover readily from illness, depression, adversity, or the like; buoyancy" (Resilience, n.d.). Having the ability to adapt to change is a skill necessary for survival in today's workplace settings. Priorities change overnight, and the ability to adjust to those changes is essential. It is also important that we spend as much time talking about stability and mental health as we do about opportunities in academia. Realistically, the rigors and processes of academia look different contingent upon one's identity and cultural background. In talking to librarians from underrepresented groups, they commonly share that they have either contemplated exiting or already left librarianship because of the way they were treated by their colleagues. Academia is not necessarily inherently safe or welcoming for those outside of the majority. A strategy that hiring managers might use is to try to put themselves in the other person's shoes. It is difficult to understand what it feels like to be "the only one" if you have never been in that position. When you are the person who identifies as being the minority, you may tend to hide your true feelings to fit in, to gain acceptance from colleagues, or to avoid being seen as hostile. In a foreword preceding the article by Caver and Livers (2002), the editors of the *Harvard Business Review* say,

> It's easy to assume that other people experience the world in the way we do. More specifically, it's very easy for white managers to assume that their colleagues of color face the same basic set of challenges they do. One level that's true: The work itself is the same. African American and other non-white managers have to make their numbers, motivate employees, hire and fire, and plan for the future. But on another level, these managers frequently contend with an atmosphere of tension, instability, and distrust that can be so frustrating they lose the desire to contribute fully or do their best work; they may even drop out altogether. Their bosses are simply unaware the miasma. (p. 76)

Managers are encouraged to try to see things from the perspective of their personnel from underrepresented groups. Gaining a better understanding of your staff members as individuals will likely result in better working relationships.

Written in 1896 during a tumultuous time for African Americans, Paul Laurence Dunbar's poem "We Wear the Mask" captures the reality of what it feels like to be an individual from an underrepresented group in the 2017 workforce. Though the poem describes the facade that many African Americans wear to hide their pain and frustration, it can be applied to the struggles that library personnel deal with, regardless of their specific diversity:

> We wear the mask that grins and lies,
> It hides our cheeks and shades our eyes,
> This debt we pay to human guile;
> With torn and bleeding hearts we smile,
> And mouth with myriad subtleties.
> Why should the world be over-wise,
> In counting all our tears and sighs?
> Nay, let them only see us, while
> We wear the mask.
> We smile, but, O great Christ, our cries
> To thee from tortured souls arise.
> We sing, but oh the clay is vile
> Beneath our feet, and long the mile;
> But let the world dream otherwise,
> We wear the mask!

Mentoring

Mentoring has been proven to be an excellent retention strategy for all librarians. There are a number of benefits for the mentor-mentee relationship. Most importantly, "mentors help the new employee understand the unwritten rules of the workplace and the cultural/organizational norms" (Steele, 1997, p. 68). Diverse individuals should be encouraged to have at two types of mentors: at least one on the campus where they work and another who works at a different library. The internal mentors may assist the employee with learning "the preferred organizational communication style, assertiveness, the importance of socializing, learning when it is acceptable to refuse assignments, and creating the balance between work and home[, which] are all important rules that a mentor can help employees master" (Musser, 2001, p. 68). Diverse individuals should also be encouraged to identify a mentor who works not for the library but on the same campus and a librarian of color at another institution, even if the library has a formal mentoring program. Identifying mentors who do not work for the library will allow the librarian to receive guidance, advice, and support from a neutral party. Baildon (2017) notes many librarians and archivists of color spend a lot of time discussing workplace politics and dynamics. This type of networking allows the librarian of color to debrief, strategize, encourage, seek advice, show newer colleagues the ropes, and sometimes vent in a supportive environment.

Professional Development and Growth

Providing professional development and growth opportunities is an excellent strategy for retaining librarians of color. It is very important that diverse employees have just as many opportunities for professional development and to grow their skills as the other librarians. There are a number of training and development opportunities available to help librarians sharpen existing skills or gain new ones on a variety of topics. Opportunities specific to librarians of color include the following:

> Minnesota Institute for Early Career Librarians From Traditionally Underrepresented Groups: The University of Minnesota Libraries offers a weeklong institute for 24 early-career college and university librarians who are from traditionally underrepresented groups and are in the first three years of their professional careers. The institute focuses on the development of library leaders from diverse backgrounds. Participants will develop specific leadership abilities proven to be necessary for organizational success (Jones & Deiss, 2017).
>
> ARL Leadership and Career Development Program (LCDP): This is an 18-month program to prepare midcareer librarians from traditionally underrepresented racial and ethnic minority groups to take on increasingly demanding leadership roles in ARL libraries (Association of Research Libraries, n.d.b).

CONCLUSION

Increasing the racial and ethnic diversity in libraries is the right thing to do. Data related to workforce diversity in libraries; the changing population demographics; and the current social, cultural, and political climate affecting our communities make increasing workforce diversity in libraries essential and challenging. In this chapter, we offer six steps your library may follow to strengthen diversity recruitment efforts, including assessing the library's readiness for diversity and inclusion; thinking about the knowledge, skills, and abilities needed to support current and emerging initiatives; developing a diversity and inclusion strategic plan; assessing the organizational climate; selecting the search committee; and providing training and development opportunities for staff.

The goal of the retention plan is to develop creative and practical strategies for retaining library personnel from underrepresented groups. The retention strategies offered focus on one guiding question, *What effect will working in your library for any given time have on an individual psychologically, physiologically, and emotionally?* Creating an environment that supports this tripartite wellness and allows personnel to bring their authentic selves to work is a must. Additional strategies include encouraging personnel to build resilience, identifying multiple mentors on and off campus, and supporting professional development and growth. Hiring a diverse workforce will only work if personnel are successfully integrated in the work of the library and the campus. It is our hope that the strategies presented will assist you with diversifying your workforce, as well as supporting the creation of a safe, inclusive, and welcoming environment for potential hires.

REFERENCES

American Library Association. (2012). *Diversity counts: 2009–2010 update*. Retrieved from http://www.ala.org/aboutala/offices/diversity/diversitycounts/2009-2010update

Anaya, T., & Maxey-Harris, C. (2017). Diversity and inclusion: SPEC kit 356 (pp. 1–172). Washington, DC: Association of Research Libraries. Retrieved from https://publica tions.arl.org/Diversity-Inclusion-SPEC-Kit-356/

Association of Research Libraries. (n.d.a). About. Retrieved October 6, 2018, from https:// www.climatequal.org/about

Association of Research Libraries. (n.d.b). Leadership and career development program (LCDP). Retrieved September 15, 2017, from http://www.arl.org/focus-areas/arl-academy/ leadership-development-programs/leadership-career-development-program#.Wb64K9OG OL8

Baildon, M. (2017). Can you be a "troublemaker" without "making trouble"? Reflections on self-development, self-acceptance, and unsettling the racialized workplace in the most productive possible way. In A. Olivas (Ed.), *Choosing to lead: The motivational factors of underrepresented minority librarians in higher education* (pp. 47–68). Chicago: Association of College and Research Libraries. Retrieved from https://ebookcentral-proquest -com.libproxy.lib.unc.edu

Caver, K. A., & Livers, A. B. (2002). Dear White boss. Do you remember that first management-team offsite? *Harvard Business Review, 80*(11), 76–81, 133.

De Pree, M. (1987). *Leadership is an art*. East Lansing: Michigan State University Press.

Elmer, V. (2012, November 29). Now hiring. Wanted? Someone just like me. Retrieved September 14, 2018, from http://fortune.com/2012/11/29/now-hiring-wanted-someone-just-like-me/

Jones, D., & Deiss, K. (2017). Minnesota Institute for Early Career Librarians From Traditionally Underrepresented Groups. Retrieved September 15, 2017, from https:// www.lib.umn.edu/sed/institute

Lowry, C. (2011). Subcultures and values in academic libraries: What does ClimateQUAL research tell us? In *Proceedings of the 9th Northumbria International Conference on Performance Measurement in Libraries and Information Services Proving Value in Challenging Times* (pp. 221–228). Heslington, UK: University of York. Retrieved from https:// www.libqual.org/documents/LibQual/publications/2013/9th_Northumbria_Conference _Proceedings.pdf

Lowry, C., & Hanges, P. (2008). What is the healthy organization? Organizational climate and diversity assessment: A research partnership. *Portal: Libraries and the Academy, 8*(1), 1–5. Retrieved from https://doi.org/10.1353/pla.2008.0010

Musser, L. R. (2001). Effective retention strategies for diverse employees. *Journal of Library Administration, 33*(1–2), 63–72. Retrieved from https://doi.org/10.1300/J111v33n01_06

Neely, T. Y., & Peterson, L. (2007). Achieving racial and ethnic diversity among academic and research librarians: The recruitment, retention, and advancement of librarians of color—a white paper, commissioned by the ACRL Board of Directors Diversity Task Force, a subgroup of the ACRL Board of Directors. 1–37. Retrieved from http://www.ala.org/acrl/sites/ala.org.acrl/files/content/publications/whitepapers/ACRL_AchievingRacial.pdf

Perception Institute. (n.d.). Implicit bias. Retrieved September 14, 2018, from https://perception.org/research/implicit-bias/

Project Implicit. (2011). Education: Overview. Retrieved September 13, 2017, from https://implicit.harvard.edu/implicit/education.html

Resilience. (n.d.). *The American Heritage Science Dictionary*. Retrieved September 15, 2017, from https://www.dictionary.com/browse/resilience

Steele, J. (1997). Sharing the "unwritten rules" impacts retention. *Cultural Diversity at Work, 9*(6), 6, quoted by Linda Musser, Effective retention strategies for diverse employees, in *Diversity now: People, collections, and services in academic libraries*, edited by Teresa Neely and Kuang-Hwei (Janet) Lee-Smeltzer, 63–72. New York: Haworth Press, 2002.

U.S. Census Bureau. (2016). American FactFinder: Selected population profile in the United States: 2016 American community survey 1-year estimates. Generated by S. Jones and B. Murphy. Retrieved from https://factfinder.census.gov/faces/tableservices/jsf/pages/productview.xhtml?pid=ACS_16_1YR_S0201&prodType=table

Chapter Nine

Developing Cultural Competency and Sensitivity

Shaundra Walker

You got tuh go there tuh know there.

—Zora Neale Hurston

This chapter provides an introduction to cultural competence within the library profession and describes my experience developing and teaching a four-week asynchronous online course on cultural competence for academic librarians. While diversity is a popular topic of conversation within the larger society and the library profession, discussions about the knowledge, skills, and abilities required of library professionals to function and to thrive within diverse environments are not as common. Slowly but surely, the profession is coming to the realization that, if librarians and libraries are to thrive in the future, possessing cultural competence will be critical to their success.

CULTURAL COMPETENCE DEFINED

Patricia Overall (2009) was one of the first scholars to offer a definition of *cultural competence* within the library and information science (LIS) profession, referring to it as "a highly developed ability to understand and respect cultural differences and to address issues of disparity among diverse populations competently" (p. 176). Several years later, in "Diversity Standards: Cultural Competency for Academic Libraries" (2012), the Association of College and Research Libraries (ACRL) borrowed liberally from the social work profession, using the following language to define *cultural competence* as a congruent set of behaviors, attitudes, and policies that enable a person or group to work effectively in cross-cultural situations; the process by which individuals and systems respond respectfully and effectively to people of all cultures, languages, classes, races, ethnic backgrounds, religions, and other diversity factors in a manner that recognizes, affirms, and values the worth of individuals, families, and communities and protects and preserves the dignity of each. (para. 6)

WHY CULTURAL COMPETENCE IS IMPORTANT

As our nation becomes more culturally diverse, developing and maintaining cultural competence will be an essential skill for librarians, and providing culturally relevant services and resources will be important for libraries of all types. Just examining the changing demographics of the United States in comparison to the lack of progress in diversifying the library profession helps one to understand the increasing importance of cultural competence.

In 2007, the American Library Association (ALA) released *Diversity Counts*, "a comprehensive study of gender, race and age in the library profession" (para. 1). Updated in 2012, the most recent version of the study indicates that, while minimal progress was observed between the first and second versions of the study, there is much room for improvement. The percentage of credentialed librarians of color working in academic, public, school, and other libraries increased by only 1% between 2006 and 2011. Maureen Sullivan, ALA president at the time, remarked, "Although the findings show some improvement in the diversity of the library workforce, we clearly have a long way to go" (para. 6).

While diversity among credentialed librarians remains stagnant, the demographics of the United States are changing rapidly. According to the U.S. Census Bureau (2012), babies of color now outnumber non-Hispanic White babies (50.4%). During the 2014–2015 school year, minority student enrollment in public schools surpassed White enrollment for the first time (Maxwell, 2014). These data suggest that, in the future, academic libraries will serve a demographic that looks much different from its workforce, making cultural competence critical for the successful provision of services and resources.

These demographic shifts are taking place at a time when the United States is increasingly polarized. Regrettably, the academic library is a place where these tensions play out. A recent article in *Library Journal* highlighted a rash of incidents that took place within academic libraries shortly after the 2016 election, including hate speech, graffiti, and even racially motivated violence (Peet, 2017). These incidents are not limited to library practitioners; there is a growing body of research on the racialized, gendered experiences of librarians working in the field, suggesting that there is much work to be done on that front, as well (Alabi, 2015; Damasco & Hodges, 2012; Daniel, 2013; Hathcock, 2015; Swanson, Gonzales-Smith, & Tanaka, 2014).

CULTURAL COMPETENCE WITHIN LIS CURRICULA

The ALA-accredited master's degree is still considered the terminal degree for library professionals. Standard 2 (curriculum) of the "ALA Standards for Accreditation of Master's Programs in Library and Information Studies" maintains that the LIS curriculum "responds to the needs of a diverse and global society, including the needs of underserved groups" (American Library Association, 2015, p. 5). Research by LIS scholars provides perspective on how well library education programs are meeting this requirement.

Mestre (2010) documented the challenges faced by librarians who had not received cultural competency training during their LIS programs. One of the major findings of the study was that neither library school curricula nor professional development in the job setting helped participants to become culturally competent. The study also called for cultural competency training to be included as a core component of LIS curricula. Similarly, Kumasi and Hill's (2011) pilot study of LIS students revealed that students felt there was a need to "infuse cultural competence learning objectives into the LIS curriculum" (p. 260). More recent scholarship has identified "diversity levers," existing places in the LIS curriculum that are ripe for the infusion of diversity and social justice concepts (Kumasi & Manlove, 2015, p. 415).

While there is increasing promise that LIS curricula of the future will be infused with cultural competence as a key learning outcome, librarians who are already working in the field, many of whom have not been the beneficiaries of such training during their LIS graduate experiences, still need this essential skill.

DESIGN AND DEVELOPMENT OF CULTURAL COMPETENCE FOR ACADEMIC LIBRARIANS

In spring 2015, the Library Juice Academy, a company providing a host of professional development courses to librarians, sought proposals for the development of a cultural competence course for academic librarians. In response to the call, I developed a proposal for the design of a four-week asynchronous online course, anchored by the ACRL "Diversity Standards."

In addition to using the "Diversity Standards" for academic librarians, the course also relies heavily on Overall's (2009) "Building Blocks to Cultural Competence" conceptual model, which presents the development of cultural competence as a continuum. The process of becoming culturally competent begins at cultural incapacity on the lower end and progresses to cultural competency on the higher end. Cultural incapacity is evidenced by an inability to recognize one's own biases, while cultural proficiency is demonstrated by "changes in policies, standards and practices to increase opportunities for culturally diverse groups" (pp. 185–186). Self-reflection, education, travel, and other forms of professional development provide an avenue to progress from the lower end of the continuum to the ideal of cultural competence (Overall, 2009).

Professional Standards and Learning Outcomes

Because the course was to be delivered asynchronously and in consideration of Overall's (2009) cultural competence continuum, I decided to focus on professional standards and learning outcomes that would be relevant to an individual. As mentioned previously, the course uses the ACRL "Diversity Standards." Specifically, it focuses on the following standards:

- Standard 1: Cultural awareness of self and others. Librarians and library staff should develop an understanding of their own personal cultural values and beliefs as a first step in appreciating the importance of multicultural identities in the lives of people they work with and serve.
- Standard 2: Cross-cultural knowledge and skills. Librarians and library staff shall have and continue to develop specialized knowledge and understanding about the history, traditions, values, and artistic expressions of colleagues, coworkers, and major constituencies served.
- Standard 4: Development of collections, programs, and services. Libraries and library staff shall develop collections and provide programs and services that are inclusive of the needs of all persons in the community the library serves.
- Standard 5: Service delivery. Librarians and library staff shall be knowledgeable about and skillful in the use and provision of information services available in the community and broader society and shall be able to make appropriate referrals for their diverse constituencies.

The course endeavors to introduce academic librarians to the concept of cultural competence in the library and information science profession. Specifically, it was designed to assist participants with

- defining *cultural competence* as it applies within the academic library in order to explain its benefits for organizational performance and success;
- examining personal cultural values and beliefs in order to better appreciate the cultural values and beliefs of others;
- investigating strategies for applying cultural competence; and

- identifying opportunities for new or enhanced library programs, services, and resources.

Recognizing that individuals enrolled in the course come from different backgrounds and with different experiences, I made the deliberate decision to weave self-reflective activities throughout the course. In the introductory module, students are provided with theoretical information, primarily through readings and presentations, that forms the foundation of the course. The students are then asked to reflect on their reasons for enrolling in the course and what they hope to gain. Not only does this exercise help the students to consider their motivations, but also it assists the instructor in clarifying the students' intent, which helps in making appropriate adjustments to the course content as necessary.

In the second module, students examine their personal beliefs as they relate to culture and identity and have an opportunity to consider the cultural beliefs and identities of their classmates. This is achieved by completing an adapted version of an activity called "The 'I Am Me' Poem," where students reflect on and list the different aspects of their identity. The activity is designed to help students gain an understanding of the complexities of identity and how individuals may see themselves very differently from how they are perceived by others. To frame the assignment, students engage in a variety of readings from the psychology literature, as well as the LIS context. Through a combination of self-reflection and comparison and contrast, this assignment serves the dual purpose of helping students to understand the role of identity and how it is influenced by culture, varies among different people, and potentially affects service delivery.

In the next module, students are tasked with contacting their institutional research offices to learn more about the demographics of their campuses. In conjunction with this task, students identify and briefly describe campus resources that are available for diverse groups. The third module also requires students to locate resourceful individuals and community groups that are already working with diverse groups on campus. Collectively, the gathered data provides students with the foundational information they need to understand the demographics of their campuses and identify potential collaborative partners.

The course's final module requires students to engage with the library literature to identify scholars and practitioners who are involved in diversity work and find replicable examples that could be implemented in their day-to-day work. Students are charged with evaluating the program or service to determine its consistency with the ACRL "Diversity Standards." Regardless of where students are positioned within their library organizations, they leave the course with a rich resource list that can be taken back to their home institutions. This resource list will be especially beneficial for students who are already engaged in diversity work within their libraries or on their campuses.

Lessons Learned and Course Revisions

One of the most evident lessons learned through developing and teaching this course was that academic librarians bring a wide range of prior knowledge and ability into the cultural competence classroom. Some participants in the course were already engaged in some level of diversity and inclusion work and were eager to build upon their prior knowledge. Others were self-motivated and enrolled in the course of their own choosing. On occasion, students enrolled because their parent institution (college or university where employed) was engaged in a campus-wide diversity program. In a few rare instances, students enrolled because cultural competence training was a job requirement due to a mandate from either the library administration or the university, perhaps as a part of the promotion, tenure, or evaluation process. In my experience, those various motivations influenced students' engagement in the course.

I observed that teaching and learning cultural competence in an asynchronous online environment can be challenging. The first time I taught the course, students were required to publish their "I Am Me" poems within a message board where they could be read by others in the class. Several students contacted me to indicate that such public posts, even in an online environment, made them feel somewhat uncomfortable, so in other iterations of the course, students have been allowed to share their poems only with me. While the most personal aspect of the assignment was modified, students are still required to post a reflection of what they learned about themselves and a consideration of how their identity characteristics might affect their work, relative to the demographics of their institutions.

On several occasions, groups of students from the same institution enrolled in the same section of the course. Oftentimes these individuals would be members of library diversity committees or represent different departments within the same institution. Although these groups obviously anticipated finding value in going through the course together, because the course was designed for individual consumption, working with several students from the same institution proved to be challenging to me for several reasons. First and foremost, because the course relies heavily on self-reflection, students from the same institution would often be reluctant to be as transparent as they might have been if they were taking the course on an individual level. To a certain degree, the asynchronous online environment benefited the students and the course by offering a degree of anonymity, perhaps making it easier for some students to share their experiences. This effect was null and void when students from the same institution attended in one setting. Similarly, because one of the information-gathering assignments required students to work with their campus institutional research office, the posts from students from the same institution became redundant and took away from the value gained by having students from different institutions share about their respective campuses. This effect was particularly strong in smaller sections of the course and at times appeared to isolate those who were truly taking the course on an individual basis.

Recommendation

Based on my experience, it might prove useful for students to participate in a series of professional development experiences designed for cultural competence. Four weeks of asynchronous learning simply does not provide an adequate amount of time to work with students. Either a two-part course or courses for individuals and for groups would be beneficial. Additional courses could delve into standards, such as those that deal with workforce diversity, organizational dynamics, and cross-cultural leadership. Librarians who have participated in the course thus far have been primarily in nonsupervisory positions. While librarians who do not supervise others certainly need to be culturally competent to deliver the best services and resources to their constituents, academic library leaders also require competence to effectively lead changes that will be necessary in the future. As Overall (2009) acknowledges, cultural competence is exhibited by changes in policies and practices at its highest level. In order for structural processes within academic libraries to change, library leaders will need to embrace diversity and develop and maintain cultural competence.

CONCLUSION

Cultural competence is an essential skill for academic librarians. Changing demographics coupled with a lack of progress in diversifying the library profession will increase the need for this skill, as academic libraries will find themselves serving constituencies with cultural backgrounds that are vastly different from those providing services and resources. Although there are promising developments within the LIS curriculum to infuse cultural competence as a key learning outcome for future librarians, there remain a large number of practicing librarians who also need cultural competence. The four-week asynchronous cultural competence course for librarians, as described in this chapter, represents one option for building cultural competence for academic librarians.

REFERENCES

Alabi, J. (2015). Racial microaggressions in academic libraries. *Journal of Academic Librarianship, 41*(1), 47–53.

American Library Association. (2012). *Diversity counts*. Office for Diversity, Literacy, and Outreach Services. Retrieved from http://www.ala.org/aboutala/offices/diversity/diversity counts/divcounts

American Library Association. (2015, February 2). Standards for accreditation of master's programs in library and information studies. Retrieved February 21, 2018, from http://www.ala.org/educationcareers/sites/ala.org.educationcareers/files/content/standards/Standards_2015_adopted_02–02–15.pdf

Association of College and Research Libraries. (2012). Diversity standards: Cultural competency for academic libraries. Retrieved February 21, 2018, from http://www.ala.org/acrl/standards/diversity

Damasco, I., & Hodges, D. (2012). Tenure and promotion experiences of academic librarians of color. *College and Research Libraries, 73*(3), 279–301.

Daniel, D. (2013). Gender, race, and age of librarians and users have an impact on the perceived approachability of librarians. *Evidence Based Library and Information Practice, 8*(3), 73–75.

Hathcock, A. (2015, October 17). White librarianship in blackface: Diversity initiatives in LIS. Retrieved February 21, 2018, from http://www.inthelibrarywiththeleadpipe.org/2015/lis-diversity/

Kumasi, K., & Hill, R. (2011). Are we there yet? Results of a gap analysis to measure LIS students' prior knowledge and actual learning of cultural competence concepts. *Journal of Education for Library and Information Science, 52*(4), 251–264.

Kumasi, K., & Manlove, N. (2015). Finding "diversity levers" in the library and information science curriculum: A social justice imperative. *Library Trends, 64*(2), 415–443.

Maxwell, L. (2014, August 19). U.S. school enrollment hits majority-minority milestone. *Education Week*. Retrieved February 21, 2018, from http://www.edweek.org

Mestre, L. (2010). Librarians working with diverse populations: What impact does cultural competency training have on their efforts? *Journal of Academic Librarianship, 36*(6), 1–21.

Overall, P. (2009). Cultural competence: A conceptual framework for library and information science professionals. *Library Quarterly, 79*(2), 175–204.

Peet, L. (2017, January 1). Campus libraries see increase in discriminatory incidents. *Library Journal, 142*(1), 14.

Swanson, J., Gonzales-Smith, I., & Tanaka, A. (2014). Unpacking identity: Racial, ethnic, and professional identity and academic librarians of color. In N. Pagowsky & M. Rigby (Eds.), *The librarian stereotype: Deconstructing perceptions and presentations of information work* (pp. 149–173). Chicago: Association of College and Research Libraries.

U.S. Census Bureau. (2012, May 17). Most children younger than age 1 are minorities, Census Bureau reports. Retrieved February 21, 2018, from https://www.census.gov/newsroom/releases/archives/population/cb12–90.html

Chapter Ten

Professional Development as a Growth Strategy

Placedia Miller and Tanika Martin

Diversity is being invited to the party; Inclusion is being asked to dance.
—Verna Myers (2011)

The need for diversity and inclusion training may appear extraneous for some organizations and especially in public libraries, where the majority of librarians are predominantly Caucasian. "In 2010, the American Library Association's (ALA) *Diversity Counts* study found that the percentage of credentialed white librarians stood at 88%, a rather disappointing result" (ALA final report of the ALA Task Force on Equity, Diversity, and Inclusion, 2016). The ALA Task Force on Equity, Diversity, and Inclusion report affirmed that there is a lack of credentialed librarians who are people of color: "Throughout our work, this task force has been very conscious of racial biases and the ways in which both conscious and especially unconscious bias impact the diversity and inclusivity of our association and profession" (ALA final report of the ALA Task Force on Equity, Diversity, and Inclusion, 2016). The task force's final report provides a glimpse into the racial and ethnic diversity in librarianship. The findings indicate a historical correlation between the lack of diversity in libraries and the limited number of diversity-related training opportunities available for library personnel, including those working in public libraries.

Just like other types of libraries, the racial and ethnic demographic of many public libraries reflects that of librarianship, so in most cases a majority of the library planning committees are likely comprised of individuals from the dominant race. The problem with this is that the lived experience of individuals from the dominant race is typically so drastically different from people of color that it may prevent them from seeing diversity and inclusion training as a necessary competency. An unfortunate consequence of having a homogenous workforce is the potential exclusion of prominent racial and equity issues, which causes further perpetuation of current biases in librarianship. Equity, diversity, and inclusion among the ALA, the Association of College and Research Libraries (ACRL), the Association for Library Service to Children (ALSC), the Public Library Association (PLA), and the Young Adult Library Services Association (YALSA) provide a foundation for examining the potential that exists when best practices for diversity and inclusion are put into action. This is an excellent starting place for an organization to reconstruct diversity and inclusion ideologies.

DIVERSITY AMONG LIBRARY WORKERS

A factsheet from the Department of Professional Employees (DPE) "explores: library staff in the workforce, diversity within the professions, education attainment of library workers, the role of women in the professions, issues of pay and pay equity, and the union difference for library staff" (DPE, 2018). One of the DPE's most notable findings suggests that the "librarian profession suffers from a persistent lag of racial diversity that has little indication of abating" (DPE, 2018). Other statistics related to diversity show the following:

- In 2015, 84% of librarians were predominately non-Hispanic Whites. Among library assistants in 2015, nearly 74% were non-Hispanic Whites, despite the fact that library assistants and technicians increased in number.
- In 2015, just 8.5% of librarians were Black or African American, 4.8% were Hispanic or Latino, and 2.8% were Asian.
- Among all workers in education, training, and library occupations, Black and African American professionals made up 10.4% of the workforce, while Hispanics and Asians represented 9.9% and 4.5% of the education workforce, respectively.
- In 2014, 42% of librarians, 28% of library technicians, and 35% of library assistants were over the age of 55. (DPE, 2018)

DEFINING *DIVERSITY, EQUITY,* AND *INCLUSION*

All diversity, equity, and inclusion work for sustaining an organizational culture must begin with establishing and understanding what these terms mean, though their definitions are continuing to progress, depending on the organization. In 2017, the ALA Council adopted new definitions of *equity, diversity,* and *inclusion* but notes that "language can both contribute to oppression and be a tool of liberation. In recognition of the way language works, especially around these concepts, many of the words and terms will continue to evolve" (About ALA, 2018):

> **Equity** recognizes that some groups were (and are) disadvantaged in accessing educational and employment opportunities and are, therefore, underrepresented or marginalized in many organizations and institutions. The effects of that exclusion often linger systemically within organizational policies, practices, and procedures. Equity, therefore, means increasing diversity by ameliorating conditions of disadvantaged groups.
>
> **Diversity** can be defined as the sum of the ways that people are both alike and different. Visible diversity is generally those attributes or characteristics that are external. However, diversity goes beyond the external to internal characteristics that we choose to define as "invisible" diversity, which includes those characteristics and attributes that are not readily seen. When we recognize, value, and embrace diversity, we are recognizing, valuing, and embracing the uniqueness of each individual.
>
> **Inclusion** means an environment in which all individuals are treated fairly and respectfully; are valued for their distinctive skills, experiences, and perspectives; have equal access to resources and opportunities; and can contribute fully to the organization's success. (About ALA, 2018)

Creating an organizational culture that embraces change and promotes the uniqueness that individuals bring to the workplace requires an awareness of implicit biases and the barriers that they present in the environment. It is important that library personnel be introduced to the concept of implicit biases through well-developed training programs that help to identify biases and offer strategies for addressing them in library environments. Eradicating issues related to implicit biases will not happen overnight; it will require an ongoing commitment from the library's entire workforce. The library staff must be open, flexible, and willing to reach beyond the parameters of their own experiences, behaviors, attitudes, and norms in order to deliver services to a vastly changing society. Yeo and Jacobs (2006) explain, "Diversity means little if there is no understanding of how the dominant culture and ideas are articulated within our institutions and our daily library practices" (p. 5). Institutional and systemic policies and practices create a culture of normality and play a significant role in the quest for training and developing staff members to be mindful that libraries are hubs of information charged to assist users in learning, growing, and excelling in their communities

IDENTIFYING BARRIERS

There are a number of reasons diversity and inclusion training may not be offered within libraries:

- The library has not adopted a shared definition of *diversity*.
- Library personnel do not understand the full scope of what it means, or the definition is limited.
- Some library leaders may assume that ongoing diversity and inclusion training is not needed due to the racial and ethnic makeup of its staff, population served, and the political climate.
- Individual library personnel members may not be aware of their own biases and the effect those biases have on the decisions they make.
- The library may lack the fiscal resources to sponsor trainers or to develop in-house training.
- Library personnel may not have the necessary competencies to develop in-house training programs.
- Many libraries may not pursue grant funding to support diversity and inclusion training due inexperience with grant writing, or personnel may not feel empowered or supported in pursuing grant funding.
- The library may not support an environment where minorities and marginalized, underrepresented populations feel safe to share feedback without repercussion. It is important to empower marginalized groups by creating opportunities for their voices to be heard.
- There may be salary disparities for women and a lack of recruitment of minorities and the disabled. The scantiness of minorities being represented in librarianship may create repetitive opportunities for training that often fail to capture the thoughts, ideas, and experiences of the global community.

In 2017, Simmons College's School of Library and Information Science (SLIS) implemented a diversity and inclusion initiative with "the primary goal of creating an inclusive and anti-oppressive environment for all students, staff, and faculty of SLIS, including the children's literature, computer science, and library and information science degrees and programs" (Knowles, 2017). Specific goals were identified in the roadmap to assist in accomplishing their objectives. Students felt profoundly empowered by participating in the training, and including their practical concerns helped to shape important dialogue for implementing changes to the "structure of course content delivery" (Knowles, 2017).

PRACTICAL STRATEGIES

There are a variety of practical strategies that a library can implement to support a workplace that is equitable, diverse, and inclusive. Those strategies include but are not limited to the following:

- Identifying individual biases as well as stereotypes that perpetuate racism and hinder the staff from delving deeper into the issues of diversity and inclusion.
- Creating goals and action plans that articulate how feedback will be received and incorporated. The plan should also discuss how expected outcomes will be sustained.
- Cultivating a workplace that is a safe, welcoming space where people of color and marginalized groups can contribute, collaborate, lead, and learn.
- Using data from surveys, community discussions, and best practices to create training programs that increase the appeal of the organization to potential employees.
- Defining what *diversity* and *inclusion* means to an organization in order to orchestrate the development of cultural competencies.
- Revisiting white papers, roadmaps, strategic plans, guidelines, and goals to ensure accountability.
- Setting a culture of competence that challenges old library trends in order to help the staff to embrace a new direction and provide clarity to move the library forward.

Cultural Competencies

Cultural competence is defined as

> a congruent set of behaviors, attitudes and policies that enable a person or group to work effectively in cross-cultural situations; the process by which individuals and systems respond respectfully and effectively to people of all cultures, languages, classes, races, ethnic backgrounds, religions, and other diversity factors in a manner that recognizes, affirms, and values the worth of individuals, families, and communities and protects and preserves the dignity of each. (ALA, 2012)

As libraries begin to collect, analyze, and reflect on the implicit bias within their respective organizations, consideration should be given to restructuring policies, procedures, and the overall culture within the organization. However, limitations set by governmental or hierarchical decision makers could create barriers to restructuring. Advocating for these barriers to be removed can be time-consuming, but moving beyond them would allow for the re-creation of strategic plans and missions that embed the importance of diversity and inclusion within an organization's framework. As a result, opportunities would be created for increasing the organization's effectiveness, enhancing the makeup of the field, and reinforcing the foundation for future librarians to formulate success plans.

Reconstruction

Practical strategies could formulate new staff work plans, goals, programs, and services. Preparing the staff for a paradigm shift by creating cultural competencies *could* increase the offering of library services in a manner that supports the ongoing transformation of knowledge acquisition. Ongoing staff development about race relations, gender inequality, wage disparities, power, and identity via discussion, lectures, and training is a great way to ensure that skill sets are relevant. In order to foster cultural sensitivity, the staff must be empowered to examine and challenge their attitudes, behavior, thoughts, and actions. Is there a direct correlation between librarians being hired and the amount of diversity and inclusion training being offered? Balancing the dialogue for librarians as it relates to race and gender may not occur overnight, but increasing the potential to leverage the professional playing field is an invitation for welcoming diverse groups of people.

METHODS TO BREAKING BARRIERS AND CULTIVATING CHANGE

Verna Myers (2011) said, "Diversity is being invited to the party." Receiving an invitation to the party does not equate to inclusion, especially if the majority population does not recognize the absence of those who do not look like them, talk like them, and have different life experiences. A practical strategy is to intentionally engage the everyday user in meaningful dialogue to acknowledge that cultural and social differences exist yet add enrichment to the experience for both parties. To this end, opportunities for academic acceleration and knowledge acquisition are unlimited. By and large, academic and public libraries are fostering their efforts to promote diversity and inclusivity in creative ways, including programming for homeless teenagers, helping ex-offenders transition back into society, teaching seniors how to use the latest technologies, and facilitating instructional design that lends itself to different learning styles. Libraries are essential knowledge centers that aggregate and disseminate information to a variety of individuals in a manner that provokes change.

There are many professional development opportunities outside of libraries that can be used to acquire, reflect, and develop greater understanding of how to break down barriers. For instance, the White Privilege Conference allows individuals to examine their thoughts and beliefs while creating personal strategies for activism within their communities (Privilege Institute, 2017). The ARL's *Diversity and Inclusion SPEC Kit 356* report mentions the creation of library fellowships used to increase professional development and entry-level appointments for new librarians (Anaya & Maxey-Harris, 2017). The State Library of North Carolina provides to its library institutions webinars, Library Services and Technology Act (LSTA) grants funded through the Institute of Museum and Library Services, and other training. These tools can serve as catalysts for greater insight and awareness of the importance of diversity and inclusion. State libraries are a great resource in which to learn and gain knowledge of trending issues and possible resolutions. They are an excellent place for librarians to gather information and connect with other librarians from across their state. PLA offers a Leadership Academy for public librarians that provides networking, educational development, and time to reflect on internal and external customer needs (Public Library Association, 2018). WebJunction offers a diverse suite of webinars at no cost to library employees that are structured to provide time for librarians to ask questions and network with other professionals. The *Library Journal*, which is written for library personnel at all levels, is a great resource for gaining a deeper understanding of diversity, equity, and inclusion.

ALA provides many grants for fellowships, awards, and scholarships to recruit more diverse professionals or to support existing librarians. For example, the ALA Spectrum Scholarship recruits and provides scholarships to

> American Indian/Alaska Native, Asian, Black/African American, Hispanic/ Latino and Native Hawaiian/Other Pacific Islander students to assist individuals interested in obtaining a graduate degree and leadership positions within the profession and our organization. The aim is to increase the number of racially and ethnically diverse professionals working as leaders in the field of library and information science to best position libraries and institutions at the core of today's culturally-diverse communities. (ALA, 2018, May 16)

The Medical Library Association (MLA) provides multiple scholarships to support the recruitment of diverse individuals into health sciences librarianship. The Naomi C. Broering Hispanic Heritage Grant is awarded to an MLA member who has an interest in Hispanic/Latino community information services and wants to pursue a professional activity in the latest medical information services using the latest technical formats (Medical Library Association, n.d.b). In addition to this grant, MLA offers a scholarship to a minority student who is enrolled in or entering an ALA-accredited library school (Medical Library Association, n.d.c). In partnership with the National Library of Medicine, MLA supports two ALA Spectrum Scholars to assist minority individuals interested in obtaining a graduate degree and leadership positions in the profession (Medical Library Association, n.d.a).

Synergistic collaborations among public, academic, and special librarians are breeding grounds for discussion, exploration, innovation, initiation, and training to imbue practices that affect consciousness toward diversity and inclusion. For example, the Joint Council of Librarians of Color (JCLC) is a diverse platform where librarians can expand professional networks, learn and share ideas and resolutions about common issues, cultivate passion toward librarianship, and bolster leadership opportunities for people of color:

> The JCLC was formed in June 2015 as a nonprofit organization that advocates for and addresses the common needs of the American Library Association ethnic affiliates. Coming together through JCLC Inc. are the American Indian Library Association (AILA), the Asian/Pacific American Librarians Association (APALA), the Black Caucus of the American Library Association (BCA-LA), the Chinese American Librarians Association (CALA), and REFORMA: The National Association to Promote Library & Information Services to Latinos and the Spanish-speaking. (JCLC, n.d.).

The University of Michigan offers a *Diverse and Inclusive Workplace Webinar* "where public librarians can learn management skills to support workplace diversity and inclusion in a public library setting" (EdX, 2018). ACRL provides a more exhaustive list of examples of diversity and inclusion committees along with ALA. ALA's Office for Diversity, Literacy, and Outreach Services sponsors its Diversity and Inclusion Outreach Fair every year at the ALA annual conference in June. The June 2017 event, held in New Orleans, featured 33 presenters who highlighted innovative and successful library outreach initiatives and programs (ALA, 2017):

> The Fair highlights library services to underserved or underrepresented communities, including people with disabilities; people experiencing poverty and homelessness; people of color; English-language learners; gay, lesbian, bisexual and transgender people; new Americans, new and non-readers; older adults; people living in rural areas; incarcerated people and ex-offenders; and mobile library services and bookmobiles. (ALA, 2018, February 14)

ALA's midwinter meeting and annual conferences are great avenues for professional development, but budget constraints can often limit staff participation. Libraries that are unable to support staff travel to conferences should look for training opportunities closer to their home institutions. For example, the University of North Carolina at Chapel Hill provides consultations for organizations and community groups who want diversity and inclusion training in the form of workshops or for use in future staff development (Office for Diversity and Inclusion, UNC Chapel Hill, n.d.).

CONCLUSION

Developing training to increase awareness of the need for diversity is an objective deserving the attention of everyone in the field of librarianship. The benefits are multifaceted, and as libraries become more relevant to the communities in which they serve, the programs, services, and even the collections reflect a depth of appreciation for the users. A lack of minorities in librarianship discourages the reality of the need for training. When our policies don't offer a remedy for the people we exclude, it becomes easier to sweep the underlying issues of systematic racism and prejudices under the rug, conveying it as a problem that simply does not exist within the walls of the library.

When libraries assemble themselves as diversity and inclusion specialists, practitioners, and advocates, services change for both internal and external customers. To increase the impact of library services, we must be mindful of the importance of equipping library staff to serve without bias but instead as prototypes for other agencies with multidimensional populations. Research indicates that libraries will need to be creative and include diverse groups of people in order to change the dynamics of the culture. Incorporating listening sessions where different perspectives can be expressed will allow libraries to identify and slowly dissolve obstacles that hinder personal and professional development.

REFERENCES

About ALA. (2018). Retrieved from http://www.ala.org/aboutala/

American Library Association (ALA). (2012). *Diversity standards: Cultural competency for academic libraries*. Retrieved April 1, 2018, from http://www.ala.org/acrl/standards/diversity

American Library Association (ALA). (2016). *Final report of the ALA task force on equity, diversity, and inclusion*. Retrieved from http://www.ala.org/aboutala/sites/ala.org.aboutala/files/content/TFEDIFinalReport_ALA_CONNECT_0.pdf

American Library Association (ALA). (2017, June 20). 2017 ALA Diversity and Outreach Fair to celebrate inclusive outreach, diversity-in-action ideas. Retrieved September 15, 2018, from http://www.ala.org/news/press-releases/2017/06/2017-ala-diversity-outreach-fair-celebrate-inclusive-outreach-diversity

American Library Association (ALA). (2017, July 18). Defining diversity. Retrieved March 30, 2018, from http://www.ala.org/advocacy/bbooks/diversity

American Library Association (ALA). (2018, February 14). ALA Diversity and Outreach Fair. Retrieved September 15, 2018, from http://www.ala.org/aboutala/offices/diversity/diversity-outreach-fair

American Library Association (ALA). (2018, May 16). Spectrum scholarship program. Retrieved March 31, 2018, from http://www.ala.org/advocacy/spectrum

American Library Association (ALA). (2018, October 30). ODLOS glossary of terms. Retrieved September 19, 2018, from http://www.ala.org/aboutala/odlos-glossary-terms

Anaya, T., & Maxey-Harris, C. (2017, September 11). *Diversity and inclusion, SPEC kit 356*. Retrieved April 14, 2018, from https://publications.arl.org/Diversity-Inclusion-SPEC-Kit-356/

DPE. (2018). Library workers: Facts and figures. Retrieved March 31, 2018, from http://dpeaflcio.org/programs-publications/issue-fact-sheets/library-workers-facts-figures/

EdX. (2018, July 26). Managing a diverse and inclusive workplace for public libraries. Retrieved August 19, 2018, from https://www.edx.org/course/managing-a-diverse-and-inclusive-workplace-for-public-libraries

Joint Council of Librarians of Color (JCLC). (n.d.). About JCLC. Retrieved March 30, 2018, from http://www.jclcinc.org/about/

Knowles, E. C. (2017). Diversity and inclusion initiatives. Retrieved January 31, 2018, from http://www.simmons.edu/academics/schools/school-of-library-and-information-science/about/initiatives/diversity-initiatives

Medical Library Association. (n.d.a). MLA/NLM spectrum scholarship. Retrieved December 15, 2018, from https://www.mlanet.org/p/cm/ld/fid=449

Medical Library Association. (n.d.b). Naomi C. Broering Hispanic heritage grant. Retrieved December 15, 2018, from https://www.mlanet.org/page/naomi-c.-broering-hispanic-heritage-grant

Medical Library Association. (n.d.c). Scholarship for minority students. Retrieved December 15, 2018, from https://www.mlanet.org/p/cm/ld/fid=304

Myers, V. (2011). *Moving diversity forward: How to go from well-meaning to well-doing.* Chicago: American Bar Association, Center for Racial & Ethnic Diversity.

Office for Diversity and Inclusion, UNC Chapel Hill. (n.d.). Consulting services. Retrieved September 15, 2018, from https://diversity.unc.edu/education/consulting/

Privilege Institute. (2017). White privilege conference. Retrieved April 14, 2018, from https://www.whiteprivilegeconference.com/

Public Library Association. (2018, October 23). Leadership academy. Retrieved November 14, 2018, from http://www.ala.org/pla/education/inperson/leadershipacademy

WebJunction. (n.d.). Course catalog. Retrieved April 14, 2018, from http://learn.webjunction.org/course/search.php?search=diversity

Yeo, S., & Jacobs, J. R. (2006). Diversity matters? Rethinking diversity in libraries. *Counterpoise, 9*(2), 5–8. Retrieved March 30, 2018, from https://freegovinfo.info/files/diversity_counterpoise.pdf

Part III

Voices From the Field

Chapter Eleven

From Recruitment to Promotion

Fostering the Success of Librarians From Diverse Populations

Alan R. Bailey

> At the heart of the issue of building a more inclusive profession . . . is the retention and promotion of librarians from diverse backgrounds.
>
> —Joan S. Howland

On many college and university campuses across the United States, students from underrepresented populations seldom see themselves represented when visiting their campus libraries. Although the reasons these libraries lack a diverse workplace may vary, I have observed firsthand and discovered from colleagues that academic libraries often do not foster an inclusive workplace environment or pathway to success for people of color; members of the lesbian, gay, bisexual, transsexual, and queer (LGBTQ) community; librarians born in other countries; and persons from other diverse backgrounds. Diversity plans, recruitment, and retention are three primary areas academic libraries should address to create a more diverse and inclusive environment.

DIVERSITY PLANS

To create an academic library culture that passionately embraces a diverse workforce, a comprehensive, unambiguous diversity plan is the essential foundation. But even more importantly for success, the plan must be more than a mandate from the campus diversity officer; chief library administrators must be wholeheartedly committed to the plan, value the benefit of an inclusive environment, and hold everyone accountable to the diversity plan.

Without this unequivocal commitment from top administrators, the plan will simply be a futile document posted on the library's web page.

On the American Library Association's "Strategic Planning for Diversity" web page, Jody Gray (American Library Association, 2011) succinctly states,

> Creating a Diversity Plan for the library is one of the most important actions we can take to ensure that diversity and inclusion become integral to the way our institutions function, both internally and externally. Creating a diversity plan involves several steps to ensure that the institution is prepared to create a diversity plan, recognizes its role within a diverse community, and addresses diversity in a meaningful and relevant way.

Gray (American Library Association, 2011) continues by identifying six crucial components of a successful diversity plan. Those components include

1. A definition of *diversity* for the organization
2. An assessment of need or justification for the diversity plan
3. A mission or vision for the diversity of the organization
4. A statement of priorities or goals
5. A delegation of responsibilities toward achievement of the plan
6. A statement of accountability

In addition to ensuring the library adheres to the diversity plan and revisits it annually to accurately reflect the library's commitment to the plan, the committee has three primary roles: (1) advising library administrators, (2) educating and serving as a model for other library employees, and (3) organizing and participating in diversity programs (Nance-Mitchell, 1996, p. 412). While striving to create a diversity-competent workplace, an effective diversity committee is the voice of every library employee.

When asked to guide libraries through the development of a library diversity plan, I instinctively refer the inquiring individuals to two articles by Julie Biando Edwards: "Developing and Implementing a Diversity Plan at Your Academic Library" (Edwards, 2016) and "Diversity Plans for Academic Libraries: An Example From the University of Montana" (Edwards, 2015). Both articles offer an overview of diversity plans while providing the knowledge and resources necessary to create and implement an effective plan that will advance the library's diversity initiatives.

RECRUITMENT

To successfully recruit a diverse workforce, academic libraries should focus on three primary areas: (1) composition of the job advertisement, (2) attracting and obtaining a diverse pool of applicants, and (3) selecting a diverse and informed search committee.

In addition to accurately detailing the responsibilities of the position and articulating clear expectations of the selected candidate, the job announcement should be free of language that would deter librarians from diverse backgrounds from applying. Requiring "excellent interpersonal and communication skills" is quite acceptable, but requiring "mastery of the English language" or "superior verbal skills" may discourage international individuals whose first language is not English. The announcement should also truthfully reflect the library's environment. A diversity statement such as "All qualified applicants will receive consideration for employment without regard to their race/ethnicity, color, genetic information, national origin, religion, sex, sexual orientation, gender identity, age, disability, political affiliation, or veteran status" is wonderful on paper, but is it fair to mislead applicants when you know your library does not embrace non-Christians, transgendered males and females, or individuals from other countries? If diversity statements like this are required campus-wide, it is the library's responsibility to ensure all employees will be embraced, supported, and given a fair chance at retention and promotion.

Attracting and obtaining a diverse pool of applicants has been a concern for many years, and libraries must do more than simply advertise in conventional professional publications. More effective methods include

1. E-mailing job advertisements to library school deans and faculty
2. Posting position announcements on diverse LISTSERVs (i.e., American Library Association committees and roundtables, such as Asian Pacific American Librarians Association, REFORMA: The National Association to Promote Library and Information Services to Latinos and the Spanish-Speaking, Black Caucus of the American Library Association, Coretta Scott King Book Awards Committee, Diversity L-SERV, Ethnic and Multicultural Information Exchange Round Table (EMIERT), and Gay, Lesbian, Bisexual Round Table
3. Establishing contacts at conferences
4. Contacting prominent members of underrepresented populations for recommendations
5. Sending targeted mailings to potential candidates
6. Maintaining a database of prospective candidates from diverse populations (Winston & Li, 2007, pp. 70–71)

Libraries working rigorously to increase diversity will surely incorporate all six of these methods into their regular recruitment procedures. I practiced each of these approaches when I served as Joyner Library's associate director for library human resources at East Carolina University because maintaining a diverse pool of applicants was one of my top priorities. Collectively these strategies were all effective, but the four that produced the most positive relationships with potential candidates nationwide and successfully created a diverse application pool were establishing contacts at conferences, contacting prominent members of underrepresented populations, targeting potential candidates, and maintaining a database of prospective applicants. Implementing these measures and interacting regularly with these identified individuals encouraged them to consider Joyner Library as a potential place of employment. In addition to welcoming my telephone calls and e-mail messages, the potential candidates shared my contact information and employment link to vacant positions with others, routinely checked our link for new positions, and contacted me frequently to see if new vacancies were on the horizon.

The composition of an effective search committee should be as diverse as possible, and prior to reviewing applications, each member should receive Equal Employment Opportunity (EEO) and Americans With Disabilities Act (ADA) training and have knowledge of core diversity competencies as defined by the university's Office of Equity and Diversity and Department of Human Resources' employment services division. An educated and diverse search committee has a greater ability to end myths, stereotypes, and misconceptions of candidates—attributes known for preventing search committees from selecting the best people for open positions. Additionally, committee members should be knowledgeable of values-based diversity, "an appreciation of diversity that's not just based on visible characteristics and demographics, [but] . . . also about diversity in thought, diversity in approach, and diversity in ideas" (Hudson-Ward, 2014, p. 32). In my experience, exit interviews with candidates from underrepresented populations provide an opportunity to assess the effectiveness of the committee. These exit interviews should be performed by the human resources librarian or a member of the university's employee relations department to determine if greater diversification of search committees is necessary or if the committee needs further diversity education.

Many academic libraries find establishing diversity fellowships to be a useful recruitment process. These time-limited appointments provide experience not only to librarians from underrepresented populations but also to library personnel and users who equally benefit from the fellow's knowledge, background, and experiences. According to the Residency Interest Group, an interest group of the Association of College and Research Libraries (ACRL), there are currently 13 residency/fellowship programs and 36 Diversity Alliance Program Institutions in North America (Association of College and Research Libraries, 2018).

RETENTION

It should be clear that creating an inclusive workplace environment does not begin by merely hiring a librarian from a diverse population. From the first day of employment, the organizational leadership team's focus should shift from hiring qualified librarians from diverse backgrounds to building a foundation for retention and promotion. Building this foundation begins with ensuring the library is welcoming to all.

According to Howland (1999),

> Libraries across the country are aggressively recruiting and actively hiring professionals from diverse backgrounds. But once these recruits arrive to the workplace, often they are surrounded by a climate that, rather than exploiting their talents, skills, and diverse perspectives to add value to the organization, creates an atmosphere that stifles these attributes and frequently leads to less than optimal performance. (p. 7)

Academic libraries must create a climate that embraces diversity—a climate in which employees do not feel they must conform to the existing environment to be successful but are able to bring their authentic selves to the library daily and contribute positively to the success of the organization. If the library is truly committed to retaining a diverse workforce and fostering a path of success, it must remove obstacles that undeniably prevent professional growth and career advancement. This means creating an environment that values all employees. This inclusive environment must be free of microaggressions and hidden biases, two barriers known for creating cold, distant, and unfriendly workplaces, making librarians from underrepresented groups feel unappreciated and isolated.

In addition to promoting productivity and better performance, mentoring can also aid retention (Hur & Strickland, 2012). In my experience, when successfully paired with a seasoned librarian, the professional career of a librarian with less experience has been both successful and rewarding. And contrary to the beliefs of many, a librarian from an underrepresented population does not have to be mentored by a librarian from the same underrepresented group. For example, I am an African American man who owes much of my professional success to two of my three mentors (a White female from the Midwest and another White female from the South) for their knowledge, wisdom, encouragement, and patience. I will always be grateful for their eagerness and willingness to guide me into a successful career. A devoted mentor can also assist in building professional relationships; offer support with research and professional service; provide advice, constructive feedback, and crucial resources; be a confidant; and help the mentee to navigate through the tenure and promotion process. For many years, mentoring has proven to be a significant factor for retention, promotion, and long-term success in librarianship (Howland, 1999).

CONCLUSION

Although research indicates that, based on academic and financial performance, the most diverse colleges and universities are also the most highly rated institutions of higher education (Winston & Li, 2007, p. 63), the staff of academic libraries generally do not accurately reflect the university's diverse student population regarding race, sexual orientation, religion, disability, gender identity, and other protected classes.

An unwelcoming workplace climate that does not create pathways to success for individuals from underrepresented populations has been identified as one of the primary reasons academic libraries are unable to recruit and retain a diverse workforce. To eliminate this barrier, making intentional efforts to create inclusive environments is a must in providing workplaces where "no one is advantaged or disadvantaged, an environment where 'we' is everyone" (Thomas, 1990, p. 109). One effective way academic libraries can demonstrate a commitment to creating this inclusive environment is to examine their diversity plans and recruitment and retention practices. A commitment of this magnitude must begin with chief library administrators if it is expected to trickle down to every library employee, including student workers. As Andrade and Rivera (2011) express it, "Developing a diversity-competent workforce is the key to fostering a positive climate for everyone, one that supports diversity" (p. 694). Diversity plans, diversity committees, bias-free job advertisements, attracting a diverse pool of candidates, diverse search committees, exit interviews, diversity fellowships, inclusive work environments, and mentoring programs are all viable ways to recruit, retain, and provide career advancements to academic librarians from underrepresented populations.

REFERENCES

American Library Association. (2011, October). Strategic planning for diversity. Retrieved from http://www.ala.org/advocacy/diversity/workplace/diversityplanning

Andrade, R., & Rivera, A. (2011). Developing a diversity-competent workforce: The UA Libraries' experience. *Journal of Library Administration, 51*(6/7), 692–727.

Association of College and Research Libraries. (2018, November). People and programs. Retrieved from https://acrl.ala.org/residency/programs/

Edwards, J. B. (2015). Diversity plans for academic libraries: An example from the University of Montana. *Library Leadership and Management, 29*(2), 1–15.

Edwards, J. B. (2016). Developing and implementing a diversity plan at your academic library. *Library Leadership and Management, 30*(2), 1–11.

Howland, J. S. (1999). Beyond recruitment: Retention and promotion strategies to ensure diversity and success. *Library Administration and Management, 13*(1), 4–14.

Hudson-Ward, A. (2014). Eyeing the new diversity. *American Libraries, 45*(7/8), 32–35.

Hur, Y., & Strickland, R. A. (2012). Diversity management practices and understanding their adoption: Examining local governments in North Carolina. *Public Administration Quarterly, 36*(3), 380–412.

Nance-Mitchell, V. E. (1996). A multicultural library: Strategies for the twenty-first century. *College and Research Libraries, 57*(1), 405–413.

Thomas, J. R. (1990). From affirmative action to affirming diversity. *Harvard Business Review, 68*(2), 107–117.

Winston, M., & Li, H. (2007). Leadership diversity: A study of urban public libraries. *Library Quarterly, 77*(1), 61–82.

Chapter Twelve

Inside the Mind of the African American Male Librarian

Carenado Davis, Tristan Ebron, and Carl Leak

> Diversity is not about how we differ, but about embracing one another's uniqueness.
>
> —Ola Joseph

PERSPECTIVE 1

Librarianship is a field that is not discussed enough in American communities. As a result, it may often be a second career choice for many. True to form, it was not the first career choice for me. I started with the intent of majoring in athletic training. This lasted for a semester before I realized that I enjoyed history more. So, I decided to pursue a double major in history and African American studies with the hopes of becoming a teacher. Fast-forward to the second semester of my sophomore year, when I decided to join the air force ROTC and began working toward becoming an air force judge advocate general or a military lawyer. This dream was squashed once I went to Georgia to work with my cousin's husband at his law firm during spring break and saw how long his days were. Family life is very important to me, and I could not see myself working from 7:00 a.m. to 7:00 p.m. most days of the week. I wanted to have a great work-life balance.

Following that spring semester, I was hired as a work-study student at an academic library, which was the beginning of my library career. I had no clue I would still be there eight years later. The work-study position was only for the summer, so it would be completed after July 2010. However, the supervisor at the time contacted me and asked if I would like to be a student worker, and by August 2010, I was back working in the department. This job required me to assist staff with daily, routine library operations, including charging and discharging materials using the integrated library system, checking book drops, shelving materials, recording library statistics, maintaining printers on the reference floor, and helping the staff with special projects. I worked in this position from August 2010 to November 2014.

A full-time library technician position became available in the department in September 2014. I was 24 at the time, so I thought, *Why not apply and at least learn how professional interviews work?* That sunny day in September, I made sure that I dressed the part. When picking what I was going to wear, I looked to one of the supervisors who seemed to always have on a white-collar shirt, tie, and slacks every day. So for my interview, I had on gray slacks, a white-collar shirt, a blue and red tie, and a red cardigan. This is an example of assimilation. On the Friday before the official interview, I had gotten two strand twists to start my dreadlock journey, but because of the typical stereotypes, I took them out and got a fade. This should not have been what I felt I had to do, but this is the understood protocol that many African Americans go through. We feel as though our natural hair is looked down upon, so we assimilate. However, we should all be allowed to express ourselves, reasonably of course. After all, it is just hair.

In fact, I had called one of my older brothers, who instructed me to take out the two strand twists for now, and once I had the job and had worked the position for a few years, then I could start them again. So that is exactly what I did. But I should not have had to do that, and I will never know if the two strand twists would have made a difference in getting hired. I should not have even felt that it may have been an issue, but this is the bigger problem in our society. People cannot be comfortable with who they are, so they assimilate in hopes of impressing others or appearing how others would want them to instead of being themselves. Would my dreadlocks be accepted as easily as a Caucasian male with a long ponytail? Sadly, I would venture to say that my twists would likely be less acceptable than the ponytail of my Caucasian counterpart. And that would be unfortunate because both should be accepted equally.

Librarianship can be a very rewarding and fulfilling career, both financially and mentally, even though many of us had other professional aspirations and goals in mind. This is usually the conversation where most information professionals can relate. One of the beautiful things about librarianship is that you can pair a master's in library science (MLS) with a degree from almost any other career or discipline and have success. Individuals interested in teaching can pair their MLS with an instructional design degree to bolster their teaching practices. Those interested in law librarianship will find the combination of an MLS and juris doctor (JD) degree necessary.

Lastly, programs that award degrees in library and information studies should make a more concerted effort to recruit individuals from traditionally underrepresented groups. There are so many people, not just minorities, who have no clue about the career options that are possible with the MLS. As for me, I am currently pursuing an MLS at North Carolina Central University in Durham, North Carolina, the only historically Black college and university (HBCU) that currently has a school of library and information science. I am proud of the fact that I am getting my degree at an HBCU and even prouder that I am joining a discipline that will allow me to pursue my passion for helping people. One of my long-term goals is to become a library administrator, a role that would allow me to add to the number of African American males in leadership roles while helping to change the face of librarianship.

PERSPECTIVE 2

I have been a librarian for 12 years. I was an English major and became interested in librarianship almost by accident while employed as a work-study student at a university library. Initially, I did not have any intentions of pursuing a career in library science. One day I stumbled across the systems department, where I learned about the library's information technology operation. I had not been exposed to this side of the library before, but it stirred my curiosity about librarianship as a profession. After completing my undergraduate degree, I was certain that I wanted to work in the library, leading me to enroll in library school. While in library school, I developed a false sense of opportunity in alternative environments beyond academic libraries. Unfortunately, those possibilities never panned out. I was hopeful early in my career, but without mentorship and guidance, I was not able to take advantage of opportunities that presented themselves.

Throughout my career I have noticed there are differences in the "acceptable standard" that places my colleagues and me on uneven playing fields, whether that is in dress or in attitude. In a previous position, I was the only Black librarian on staff. I noticed that my colleagues would dress down (jeans) when working on the weekends, so I followed suit. Inevitably, my colleagues would have more students come to them with questions on the weekends. Conversely, students would approach me for assistance on days that I came to work wearing dressier attire. Apparently, there was an unspoken assumption that I was not as competent as my colleagues when I dressed down, and to be seen as equally competent, I had to be dressed more professionally.

This assumption spans professional conferences and meetings, as well. If I dress more casually, it is assumed that I am not a part of the environment, but when I dress up, it is assumed that I belong, even though my colleagues are assumed to be a part regardless of how casual or professional they dress. There seems to be an underlying stigma that Black men in the field are not allowed to have a mediocre or bad day. There is this expectation that we have to be at the very top in performance, appearance, and intellect to even be considered as competent as our White colleagues who may not be representing themselves with the same standards. Oftentimes, other Black colleagues and I are seen as the "fun bunch" and not professionals. What is perceived as more professional behavior could be perceived by colleagues as being aggressive or angry. This fine line has affected how I negotiate because I do not want to lose out on opportunities, settle for less, or be perceived as a problem or stereotypical Black male.

My personal career growth has suffered because of issues with diversity and inclusion in the library field. I have worked at both HBCUs and predominantly White universities. Initially I had to overcome the thought that I would not be taken as seriously by working at an HBCU as I would if I had worked at a predominantly White university. I now know that this was imposter syndrome from both a personal and an institutional perspective. It also affected how I applied for future opportunities. I was once overlooked for a position that I was well qualified for and for which I had already been performing the duties.

The hiring practices of libraries have to be evaluated, especially when it comes to Black male librarians and opportunities for advancement or leadership. Libraries must continue to recruit underrepresented minorities. As the only minority on a staff of approximately 30, I've found myself fostering feelings of social isolation and having to overcompensate. I find it difficult to bring my authentic self to work because there are assumptions about me as a Black man that are not palatable for my White colleagues. I think that my colleagues have good intentions but do not share my experiences socially, professionally, and culturally. This plays into me not being comfortable being fully open in my identity. There is an unspoken, unrealistic expectation for me to be perfect with no room for error. If I make a mistake in my diction or performance, I am perceived as not being qualified for the job I hold. The field of librarianship is definitely lagging behind in its progress toward diversity and inclusion and has a long way to go.

PERSPECTIVE 3

I have worked in libraries for nearly two decades. When I first began my career in librarianship, I only knew of one Black male librarian, and since that time, progress has been slow in recruiting. I can still count on my hands in single digits the number of Black male librarians whom I know of in the profession across all of the networks that I have access to.

I was into technology and on pace once I graduated with my undergraduate degree to go work in the technology sector when I stumbled upon librarianship as a career. While in school, I was employed as a work-study student in the IT department. This is where I saw how the library infrastructure was held together with networks, databases, and coding. It sparked my interest because I had a stereotypical view of librarianship (older White lady who sat at a desk, checked out books, and shushed library patrons) before that moment. Because of this perspective, I had not found librarianship remotely interesting or considered it as an option for a career. Through working in the IT department, I gained a new career perspective and attended North Carolina Central University for library school. Unfortunately, even though I was attending an HBCU, as an African American man, I was still a minority.

As my career progressed in librarianship, I discovered that I would be the minority more often than not. I have found myself in library environments where I am not only the lone male but also the lone minority person on the entire library staff. These situations have caused me to feel isolated and alone in the profession. This isolation was compounded by the fact that I did not have any mentors who looked like me whom I could look to for guidance or support. Many times, I felt alone when dealing with issues and anxieties of work life and microaggressions associated with colleagues not empathetic to what I was going through.

There have been many instances where my Caucasian colleagues have stereotyped me based on assumptions about African American men that are not true. This has caused me to not feel comfortable being myself around my colleagues. There seems to be this unspoken set of standards for my Caucasian colleagues and another set for minority colleagues. For example, some of my colleagues can do just the basics of their jobs and have average performances but are seen as superstars and leaders and then are promoted. Conversely, I have to perform exponentially above what they are doing, have additional degrees, engage in professional development activities, and garner awards and accolades just to be seen as almost as competent as my counterparts.

As an African American male librarian, it is important for library administrators and colleagues to put forth the effort to understand, recruit, and retain minorities in the field of librarianship. I have worked at various types of libraries during my career, and in all of those settings, one thing was always consistent. I always felt I had to prove my value and qualifications to show that I was supposed to be there. I never felt that my White colleagues had that same burden. For example, whenever I attend meetings outside of the library, I have to wear my name tag stating who I am and what area I represent. I also have to dress far above what my colleagues deem professional. Otherwise, I am looked at with questions of, why are you here, or do you belong here? My White colleagues never get questioning looks about whether they belong in a certain place or are supposed to be at a meeting, regardless of how they dress or whether they are wearing a meeting badge.

It is these types of interactions that continue to hinder progress toward true diversity. I have also had the experience of my White colleagues mapping out how my career should look based on their perspective of me without asking me or considering the plans I already have. These negative interactions affect our self-identity as minority librarians when it is already difficult for us to be ourselves in the workplace. To have our thoughts and feelings neglected, ignored, and reimagined for us perpetuates an identity crisis. It creates a plight around self-worth and value.

As a minority male in the library environment, opportunity, guidance, benefit of the doubt, mentorship, and cultural support have not been available to me and other minorities at the same level or frequency as my Caucasian colleagues. I do not think the challenges that I have faced in my career have been intentional. I think it comes down to a lack of understanding and empathy and not having intentional conversations and systems in place to address issues of diversity and inclusion for underrepresented minorities. Libraries across the profession need to be strategic in how minorities are recruited, retained, and made to feel welcome and comfortable being themselves.

Chapter Thirteen

Interpersonal Relationships With Minority Women in Leadership Positions

kYmberly Keeton

Always be smarter than the people that hire you.

—Lena Horne

JOURNAL ENTRY: ALLOW ME TO INTRODUCE MYSELF

I am an African American writer and art librarian. This chapter describes the experiences that led me to walk away from a workplace that I characterize as beautiful chaos. It is my hope that sharing my story will encourage other African American women to tell their own stories about personal experiences they have encountered in librarianship.

The year 2014 was a momentous year for me. In May 2014, I graduated with a master of library science (MLS) and then accepted my first professional position as an academic librarian in October of that year. When I began my position, the library was under the leadership of an African American female. I was excited to be working for a library at a historically Black college and university (HBCU). As someone who aspires to become a library leader, I was excited to be working at a library that was led by an individual whose intersectionalities were similar to my own—female and African American.

This feeling of excitement dissipated once I realized she was not a credentialed librarian, did not have previous experience working in or leading a library, had not completed any formal leadership-development training, and lacked an interest in mentoring me or my colleagues. Taken all together, I believe the aforementioned items may have affected her ability to lead the library. It was unfortunate that, under her tenure, I would not learn to be the type of leader that I wanted to become.

This experience awakened in me a desire to investigate the experiences of women minorities, particularly African American women, who hold leadership roles in librarianship. One can't underestimate the importance of professional development and training in mentoring, interpersonal dynamics, motivating others, and thriving among those who share your same skin color.

AFRICAN AMERICAN WOMEN LEADERS IN ACADEMIC LIBRARIANSHIP

The training, guidance, and relationship formed with my closest mentor, also a minority female, put me on a different plateau before entering the library profession. For example, she informed me early on about the importance of knowing whether I wanted to work in a special, academic, school, or public library. Thanks to her guidance and encouragement, I earned the MLS and began my career as an academic librarian. Having just earned the MLS, I was confident in the knowledge and skills that I brought to my first position. During my first year as an academic librarian, I achieved a number of accomplishments, including establishing myself as a personable librarian, creating an information literacy program focused on the arts, introducing new course offerings to the campus, writing scholarly articles and book chapters, collaborating with faculty members from a variety of disciplines, and serving on the faculty senate.

I believe these items positively supported the library's mission while introducing an innovative approach to the use of library collections and resources in the university's arts-related curriculums. My work on campus resulted in me being a sought-after collaborator by the faculty and a trusted advisor by the students. I was extremely enthusiastic and proud of the work I was doing on behalf of the library. I was hopeful that the library's leadership shared this sentiment. Instead, it appeared to me that the library's leadership might have felt threatened by my activities and those of others who were trying to be innovative and progressive.

I began my investigation of minority women in leadership with a literature search but found very few articles that addressed the topic. Sandra K. Epps (2008) echoes my sentiments about the lack of literature regarding development of minority leadership in libraries when she states, "Library literature of the past 20 years has very little research specifically related to the development of minorities in leadership" (p. 256). After reading this article, I wondered if African American women in library leadership positions are provided professional development opportunities to enhance their leadership abilities.

The motivating factor for my decision to leave a position I loved was related to the process the university used to hire the new director. The library faculty was not included in the search process for the library director vacancy, a disappointing decision made by the institution's leadership. I felt let down by this decision, and my exposure to what I felt was a toxic environment early on pushed me to think about my future as a leader.

AFRICAN AMERICAN WOMEN IN MANAGERIAL OR EXECUTIVE ROLES

I was disappointed to learn that the university leadership appointed the interim director to the directorship without any input from the library staff. Working for someone who had limited knowledge about my work as a librarian or the role the library plays at a university was challenging. I soon realized that working for this institution no longer aligned with my professional values. To counteract these feelings, I sought out mentors to help guide me through the socialization process in various settings as a professional librarian. I found that mentors and allies who were external to my institution provided invaluable insight that would help me work through the difficult situation I was experiencing. Allies are extremely important to African Americans who are trying to maneuver in academic librarianship.

THE IMPORTANCE OF MENTORS IN ACADEMIC AND SPECIAL LIBRARIES

According to authors in a study prior to the 21st century, a small portion of research attests to African American women in academic administration and less research discusses the role of mentors and sponsors in their professional careers (Allen, Jacobson, & Lomotey, 1995). In my short time in the profession, I have only met one African American librarian who has taken the time to mentor me and did not see it as a chore. She has served as my mentor and trusted advisor since 2016, believing in my abilities, consistently sharing information, and helping propel my career to the next level. I am grateful for her commitment to mentoring new leaders, especially women of color. Working with her has helped to restore my passion for working in libraries.

By no means am I suggesting there are no African American women in leadership roles who are mentoring African American women, but the sheer numbers of African American women in the profession are dismal. In 2006, the American Library Association published a comprehensive study entitled *Diversity Counts*, about race, inclusion, ageism, and gender. Here is the embedded code language (italicized) that I mix-mastered through my brown eyes: "While credentialed *librarians remain* predominantly *female* and *white*, this new *data provides* a *fuller picture of* diversity within the *profession today*" (American Library Association, 2007). The real picture revealed that there were 118,667 credentialed librarians in the profession, and out of that number, there were only 6,160 African Americans (American Library Association, 2007).

African American women are sprinkles of history within librarianship. We should strive to document our legacies for the next generations coming after us. It is only through my faith and spiritual belief in God that I have made it thus far and have not walked away from librarianship.

CLINGING ON TO FAITH AND SPIRITUALLY IN ACADEMIC LIBRARIANSHIP

I agree with Shirley Walker's (2009) assessment that African American women cling to faith and spirituality to face the clichés, myths, and syndromes made up by society to refute the power and right for African American women—whose ancestors paid for them to be included—to exist in White roles (p. 652). Praying daily was all I had to keep me going during my first two years as a librarian. In a span of two months, I lost my mother and then my aunt. It was a devastating blow to my heart, mind, soul, and spirit. I had no one to confide in at work, and I felt I was part of a downsizing agenda. I am grateful that my personal village introduced me to my homey Jesus. The cool part about our relationship is that he penned me/us/we/you a verse (John 15:15, KJV): "Henceforth I call you not servants; for the servant knoweth not what his lord doeth; but I have called you friends; for all things that I have heard of my Father I have made known unto you."

Jesus's friendship manifested in more ways than one in my life at the institution where I worked. Though I am an African American woman, I am aware and have learned through trial and error that there are not always people within my own culture who are for the good of my people. My experience is a testament that the value of libraries and what they mean to the students, the faculty, and the community is not always recognized. Every story ends, and this one did, too. I decided to walk away from a place that was no longer for me. Once the chapter was closed, I was able to grieve, see my own mistakes, and not be bitter. Nothing in my life is one-sided. I had to look in the mirror, too, in order to be able to look back at what I did not want to become in the present or future.

JOURNAL ENTRY: THE ARTICULATED
CONCLUSION ABOUT MY JOURNEY

I understand that what I went through was a teaching lesson in ethics, leadership, and continued growth as a human being. This is the message I want to convey in this short soliloquy of sorts: There is no way that there will be a diverse workforce if we cannot first treat each other with respect, appreciate other people's successes, and empower each other to embrace our individual uniqueness. I remember wondering why in an interview I was asked if I could motivate others. I now understand the genesis of this question, as it takes a special person to be a librarian and a leader. I learned many lessons from this experience that I share with new minority librarians:

1. Always be cognizant of the workplace culture of your library. Keep in mind there will likely be multiple cultures at play: the university, the library, your department, and so forth.
2. Work diligently to gain an understanding of the value that the library plays on your campus or in your community.
3. Do not let anyone pressure you into taking on an administrative role if you are not comfortable doing that or if your library is not willing or able to invest in helping you develop your leadership skills. You don't have to be an administrator to lead others. It takes a village to manage a village, but do not take that lightly. It is also okay just to follow.

The most significant lesson I learned from this situation is that it is okay to leave a toxic environment. So, if you are working in a toxic environment, the best thing you can do for yourself is to begin working on your exit strategy. I decided to put my entrepreneurial skills to work while I sought employment elsewhere rather than staying in a situation that was not working. There are not enough pages allotted for me to explain the totality of the situation, but I learned from it and have progressed mentally, spiritually, and professionally. I am still working on me, too. I do believe that all women need to strengthen their leadership competencies. Conversely, the libraries should be prepared to provide the funding support and the release time needed to allow leaders to pursue professional development opportunities. I'll end with this thought: It may take you years to learn about who you are and accept everything about your being, but it takes seconds to judge someone else. Being smarter than the people who hire you means that you can chart your own path.

REFERENCES

Allen, K., Jacobson, S., & Lomotey, K. (1995). African American women in educational administration: The importance of mentors and sponsors. *Journal of Negro Education, 64*(4), 409–422.

American Library Association. (2007). *Diversity counts*. Retrieved from http://www.ala.org/aboutala/offices/diversity/diversitycounts/divcounts

Epps, S. K. (2008). African American women leaders in academic research libraries. *Libraries and the Academy, 8*(3), 255–272. doi:https://doi.org/10.1353/pla.0.001

Walker, S. A. (2009). Reflections on leadership from the perspective of an African American woman of faith. *Advancing in Developing Human Resources, 11*(5), 647–656.

Chapter Fourteen

Otherness, Inclusion, and Libraries

Sonia Alcantara-Antoine

She was all of these things and of something more that did not come from the Rommelys nor the Nolans, the reading, the observing, the living from day to day. It was something that had been born into her and her only . . . the one different thing such as that which makes no two fingerprints on the face of the earth alike.

—Betty Smith, *A Tree Grows in Brooklyn*

Libraries have been a welcome haven to me. I grew up as a Dominicana in predominantly White communities on Long Island, New York. Growing up, I always felt like an odd duck, an "other" who was different from everyone else and who did not quite fit in. My otherness was a cross I bore throughout my childhood until I learned to embrace it and celebrate it, unapologetically and with pride. Unwittingly it propelled me toward libraries, whose emphasis on inclusion and diversity ensured that I would be a welcome addition to its ranks.

My path to librarianship started with the funny papers. My father read the comics to me out of the *Newsday* newspaper. My favorite day of the week was Sunday, when the comics were bright and colorful. The larger size of the comic strips made them seem three-dimensional, as if they jumped off the page and came to life. I enjoyed the pseudoseriousness of *Garfield* and *Peanuts* and was intrigued by the high school melodrama of *Archie*, which seemed like a world apart from my own.

I do not remember my father doing different voices for the characters—he wasn't a playful type of man—but I do remember, quite vividly, the act of him reading to me. He would patiently read to me anytime, anywhere, on demand. During breakfast, I sat on his lap with a newspaper between us. During bath time, he perched on the rim of the tub with the comics section folded in his big hands while I splashed in the water. My father opened my mind and exposed me to a world of words, language, imagination, and ideas.

Reading was the norm in my household. My parents had immigrated to the United States from the Dominican Republic in the 1960s. My mother read the Bible and religious books in Spanish. My father was a thoughtful and intelligent man who favored the daily newspaper or a Stephen King paperback. By elementary school, I was an avid reader like my parents. *Reading Rainbow* was one of my favorite TV shows. I would sing the theme song gleefully each time it came on the air: "*Butterflies in the sky . . . I can go twice as high! Take a look, it's in a book, a reading rainbooooww!*"

All the reading material we had in the home was purchased or subscribed to by my parents. Public libraries as we know them to be in the United States did not exist in the Dominican Republic when my parents were growing up in the 1940s and 1950s. Because my parents were not familiar with how libraries operated in the United States, it did not occur to them to seek one out for themselves or their children. I ended up discovering libraries on my own. I recall going on a class field trip to my local public library when I was in elementary school. It was large and cavernous, with dim lighting. As a shy, introverted kid, the building frightened and overwhelmed me. I could not explain this to my parents because they had never been there, nor was it within their realm of awareness. My elementary school library by comparison was small, tidy, and bright. I felt safe there and could easily explore the small space without feeling dazed and lost. It was made for a shy, quiet girl like me with a curious mind. All those books lining the shelves filled me with awe. I had never seen so many books for kids in one place, and it felt as if I was given an invitation to open them all and explore. It represented countless stories to be told and heard and infinite possibilities.

I read voraciously as a child, even sneaking books to read during Sunday church service. I found comfort in books as my parents' relationship imploded. I was shy and socially awkward but found kinship and understanding through books. My elementary school participated in an annual book mail-order program where kids could purchase books from a catalog. I was excited to receive the catalog and curated my book wish list with the same intensity as I did my annual Christmas lists to Santa. I would give my father the list, he would write the school a check, and a short while later, I would receive a stack of books that were my very own.

Back then, I was captivated by the saccharine tragedies of Lurlene McDaniel where the heroines were struggling with debilitating and sometimes life-threatening illnesses. I was a healthy kid, and no one in my family was sick, but I identified with the protagonists, who were different from everyone else and had to survive adversity. I attended a predominantly White elementary school and was only one of three kids who was not White. I was an "other" myself, and it was the otherness of the characters that I connected with.

When I got older, I picked up my father's dog-eared Stephen King paperbacks like *Thinner* and *Misery* and enjoyed the Victorian soap operas of Charles Dickens, such as *Great Expectations* and *Hard Times*. As a first-generation American, I gravitated toward stories about the immigrant experience, such as Betty Smith's *A Tree Grows in Brooklyn*.

The characters in these books were almost exclusively Caucasian, and many of the stories I read did not mirror my own life. I did not notice until later in my teens and twenties that I was rarely represented in the books that I read, either on the covers or within the pages. Books were an escape and a window to look into, even though I was on the outside looking in. The things that preoccupied me, such as whether my parents could afford to buy me the trendiest clothes or how I was mortified to be seen riding in my mom's beat-up car, were not reflected in the stories that I read. The fact that I often had to translate official communications from the school for my mom or that we only owned a Spanish dictionary that I used to cleverly reverse-engineer the definitions to complete my vocabulary homework, was not reflected in what I read. The stories did not relate to how my parents could not afford to buy me braces, which I desperately needed to correct my diastema (a gap between the teeth). I did not read about characters who looked like me, with brown skin and a curvy body, or who grew up thinking they were fat because they did not look like the thin and wispy idea of beauty embraced by their White peers. I felt like an "other," conspicuously so, or as my mom would say "la mosca en el vaso de leche," which translated means "a fly in a cup of milk."

There is a sense of alienation that comes with being a person of color in a predominantly White community. There is another, more acute sense of isolation that comes from not quite fitting in with those who do look like you. As a Latinx with a caramel-brown complexion, I never felt Dominican enough for the light-skinned Dominicans at my high school. I could speak Spanish but sucked at dancing merengue and bachata. I was the product of African slaves brought to the Americas, but I wasn't African American. I was most comfortable reading books and enjoyed school, but being bookish and smart was not readily embraced in either culture. I was an "other" straddling two cultural identities, being both and neither.

Eventually I felt less alone when I began to read books written by writers who looked like me and were about people whose lives were reminiscent of my own. My literary explorations expanded to include Julia Alvarez, Isabel Allende, Toni Morrison, and Esmeralda Santiago. Later in college, I devoured history about the Harlem Renaissance and dove deep into a research project about Blaxploitation films for a class about representation of people of color in film. I was fascinated by all that I read and learned about. I compared what I read to what I had been exposed to in earlier readings. I started to create a new narrative for myself, one in which I was not an "other."

My first job as a page at my local public library was a refuge for me. I enjoyed flipping through the books before I shelved them. It was a quiet, dreamy place where I could just be myself, comfortable in my own skin and surrounded by books. After struggling with otherness my whole life, this place felt safe. It was here that I began to experience what inclusion looked and felt like. Here, I did not have to justify or explain my love of books. Here, I could be shy, socially awkward, and nerdy. I saw that the library was a haven for many. While my community wasn't particularly diverse, I saw it was a place that anyone could use, free of charge, and read about anything they wanted, free of judgment. I saw that the library created a sense of community and belonging for others like me who had never felt that before.

I took a gap year after high school because I struggled with figuring out my next chapter. By comparison, my Caucasian high school friends were frighteningly driven and sure-footed. They would graduate from high school in 1996 and from college by 2000 and were confident of future careers in medicine and law. As for me, I was smart and had always been a good student. I knew that college would be the next logical step for me, but I did not know how to get there. No one in my immediate family had been to college. I applied and got accepted into New York University, but the tuition was astronomical. How would I pay for college, knowing that my parents could not afford it? Growing up, I had never even slept over at a friend's house (Dominican parents aren't usually down with their kids sleeping in a stranger's house). So how would I survive living in a dorm? How would I get around if I did not own a car? I was plagued with uncertainty and doubt.

I ended up going to community college first and eventually a public university. Both were affordable and safe because I got to live at home and stay close to my mom. I worked full time throughout, paying for the classes that would eventually lead to a bachelor's degree in English. However, my path through undergraduate education was meandering and desultory. I struggled to find a career path that matched my burgeoning sense of self.

I considered careers in education and psychology, as well as journalism and nutrition. I briefly entertained being a writer but knew I did not have the gift to be like the writers I admired. I imagined myself traveling the world and helping others on an exotic Peace Corps mission. A couple of my professors encouraged me to earn a PhD in American literature so I could be a professor like them. Nothing was the right fit, so I took my time earning my bachelor's degree, stalling for time until I could figure out what I would be when I grew up. In my final semester of my senior year, I still had not figured it out. I was determined not to graduate without a definitive career path. I visited my school's career counselor and took a couple of career aptitude and personality tests. To my surprise, one of the suggested careers was *librarian*.

Libraries had always been in the back of my mind, ever since my first job as a library page. But all I knew of that experience was that I could be a children's librarian or a reference librarian, and I did not want that for the rest of my life. Nevertheless, I did some homework.

I looked at the American Library Association (ALA) website and read a few articles online. What I read surprised me. Libraries had evolved significantly in the few years since I had worked in one. There were many paths within libraries, including numerous types of libraries and many types of jobs that required more than sitting behind a reference desk. Libraries were just as much about technology as they were about books. They championed intellectual freedom, civil discourse, and lifelong learning. Libraries were vanguards of social justice, giving people a leg up in life and defending free, unfettered access to information. Furthermore, libraries were in a state of transformation and reinvention, and that excited me. As a Brown girl who grew up loving words, ideas, and learning, I knew that libraries would be a good home for me because I wanted the same for others.

I spoke with a trusted professor about libraries and possibly becoming a librarian. I was pleasantly surprised to learn that his wife was a librarian. This thing that I wanted to do was not so strange or far-fetched. When I eventually decided to pursue librarianship, I was met with odd approval from my family. No one in my family was a librarian, and no one quite understood why this was my career choice. My mother's only concern was that I stay out of trouble and work hard at a good-paying job. My father understood and supported my aspirations for higher learning, but librarianship? Why get a master's in that when there were more laudable options? It was as if I had a dazzling career ahead of me as a navy SEAL or an FBI agent, and I gave it all up to be the local dogcatcher.

I persisted, nevertheless, knowing that this was the right career path for me. I got a paraprofessional position at my local public library, and subsequently I got accepted to attend the MLS program at Florida State University. After many aimless years, I finally had a purpose and specific career goals. I felt relieved. However, I looked around the library where I worked, and I was only one of five people of color. The community we served was diverse, including significant pockets of patrons who struggled to overcome generational poverty, high illiteracy rates, and systemic racism. Most of the staff members were Caucasian, and I found them to be derisive, condescending, and insensitive to the needs of our patrons. My colleagues of color were silent or laughed along, just to get by. I wavered, wondering if this was the right move for me. Where did my values and I fit within this library system and, moreover, within this profession?

The game changer for me was when I received the American Library Association's Spectrum Scholarship. The scholarship seeks to increase representation of underrepresented groups within librarianship. As part of the scholarship, I got to attend a leadership institute, followed by my first ALA annual conference. I was in a cohort of 50 other scholars who looked like me—yellow, brown, and black. They had stories like mine and names like mine. It was emotionally impactful, and many of us cried on our last day. We were all starting out in a profession that was overwhelmingly White. But we were not alone, and there was enormous strength in that unity.

The Spectrum family has grown to more than 1,000 members, and it is wonderfully rewarding to see how the field has become more diverse over the years. We have a long, long, long way to go, but at least we are seeing some progress, however incremental. We need to look like the people we serve, particularly in public libraries. That starts with having a diverse staff who is culturally competent, committed to service, and able to meet people where they are.

A decade or so later, I am a public library director. Through my work, I seek to provide a safe space for all in my community—at all stages of life and from all walks of life—to explore, learn, and grow. Libraries provide opportunities for transformation so that every individual can live his or her best life. More importantly, they are about inclusion. All are welcome at the library, even brown-skinned Dominicanas like me.

Chapter Fifteen

An Equal Employment Opportunity Complaint in Progressive Land Library

An African American Female in Middle Management

Because I've been to the mountaintop. And I don't mind. Like anybody, I would like to live—a long life; longevity has its place. But I'm not concerned about that now. I just want to do God's will. And He's allowed me to go up to the mountain. And I've looked over. And I've seen the Promised Land. I may not get there with you.

—Martin Luther King Jr.

THE WONDER YEARS: EARLY DAYS AT THAT SYSTEM

I accepted a promotional opportunity in a nearby public library system over a decade ago. The system was in a progressive county with a great reputation for innovation and fostering a positive work environment. The county had a high cost of living, and the customer base was predominantly upper class and White. However, the county leadership boasted a great progressive and liberal outlook that celebrated and welcomed diversity and inclusion. Let's call it Progressive Land.

My salary request was met, and I felt like a revered new addition to the staff. The position allowed me to work days only and to telecommute regularly. I was happy for the opportunity and immediately set out to be dynamic and elevate the service. Though I only supervised a few staff, I was responsible for the budget, policy, and system-wide coordination of selection and collection maintenance in all formats for my service groups.

From all indications, I had a successful first few years at the Progressive Land Library System. I got excellent feedback on performance appraisals

135

and 360 surveys from my direct supervisor, peers, and direct reports. Comments included "Great interpersonal skills . . . quick learner . . . dynamic . . . energetic . . . she will be a director someday."

I met policy-writing, budgeting, and planning goals and established collegial and professional relationships with coworkers from all departments and all locations. I successfully pitched a request to my shrewd, exacting coworker for a larger share of the materials budget for my service area. I led the effort to increase digital services to the customers in the age group I served. I was a favorite to serve on hiring panels, presenting a diverse face to candidates.

Following discord in another department, a department head left the system and later recruited me to follow her. She offered expanded supervisory experience, a higher salary, and an opportunity to lead multiple service departments at a busy location in a more diverse community.

When my director learned of my offer at the system close by, she and my direct supervisor worked to retain me. They met the salary and offered me a similar opportunity to stay. The offer was a one-year swap with a coworker who wanted to try out my job in collection development. I would take a position as acting branch head. We could return to our old roles after the year. The entire arrangement was outlined in a formal letter from human resources on company letterhead. The swap came with an immediate recommendation to join a prestigious leadership program the county offered for emerging leaders. Feeling like an extremely valued darling of the system, I carefully developed a resource guide to aid my colleague in successfully carrying out her new duties for a year.

THE DESCENT INTO THE DOGHOUSE

The leadership program was challenging and rewarding. It required a special project that would affect my library based on what I learned in the cohort. This caused some tension with the head of branches, my immediate supervisor during the swap. She bristled at any change to one of "her" buildings and eventually had our head of administration inform me that I was just supposed to "keep the lights on" during the swap.

Near the end of the swap period, the head of materials management, my true supervisor, announced her retirement. In my previous appraisal she had said, "_____ is going to be the director someday. It can happen for her one day. She's going to move right along." Personally, she shared with me that I had potential for promotion and advised that I apply for her job, especially since it was coinciding with the end of my swap year.

However, it was announced that a county staff person without a library degree or any library experience was being placed temporarily into the position as head of materials management. A message was posted to our Intranet: "Her mother was a librarian, so she gets it." Even my outgoing former supervisor was chagrined to learn this. However, the official hiring process would be postponed. I was also asked if we could postpone the ending of my swap since my colleague and the department were implementing our new integrated library system (ILS). I could see the rationale in doing this, so I agreed to postpone. The director and I had lunch, and I spelled out to her that I wanted to return to management when the swap was over, and she confirmed that would indeed happen.

Next, I learned that my temporary swap assignment was going to be advertised internally. I thought they would hire someone to fill my temporary role, and I would finally get to go back to my previous position, as indicated in the written agreement that was now over six months past the agreed date. I recall seeing an urgent e-mail to all the staff encouraging them to apply, as my temporary role was closing in 24 hours. I did not apply. This was the beginning of my descent into the doghouse.

After the deadline passed, I invited my coworker to have lunch and thanked her for the swapping opportunity. I informed her that I wanted my original position in materials management back. I invited her to continue helping with selection when she returned to her former position. Since she had not applied for her former position, I said we could lobby library administration to have her join my team in materials management. She shared that she had not applied for the permanent role in her former position because she'd been told that she didn't need to, as I was expected to apply to stay in her former role. She was mortified to learn what I shared because she'd been promised that my old job would be hers! She did *not* want to return to either her original role and location or her former temporary role. I was stunned!

Within two days of this lunch meeting, I was summoned to headquarters. I was in deep trouble. I was reprimanded for not applying for the vacancy for my temporary role and for informing my colleague that I wished to swap back. The CEO and my boss during the swap considered my wish to return to my previous position as a unilateral decision that was not sanctioned. More importantly, it seemed that I had upset my colleague, who actually cried in the administrative offices. I promised that I had not been rude or forceful with her. I tried to explain my reasoning for thinking I could swap back by producing the official HR letter from my records stating the terms and conditions of the swap, but it didn't matter.

The letter presented a conundrum for them, but they recovered within a few days by offering a very murky job description of a position in a different department. It would be at the same level as my former job but with no direct reports. I learned from the head of that department that he had no idea about the position because it had never existed before. I was informed that I could either take the newly created position or apply for my temporary job to become permanent, but going back to materials management would not happen under any circumstances. Also, because I'd blown my chance to apply internally, I would be forced to compete for my job with external candidates, since they had not found any suitable internal candidates from the first search. Another staff person who'd been supervising a busy branch on Sundays applied internally but was not even interviewed.

When my interview day came, I gave what I'd considered a lackluster performance, since I felt railroaded. I found it interesting that some questions seemed to be tailored to the experience I'd had in the temporary role. For example, I was asked, "Tell us about a time you had to change workflows or service locations to more efficiently and effectively serve the customers." Sharing this information would include the very things that had not endeared me to the head of branches. I was notified and congratulated the very next day that the job—my temporary job that I didn't really want—was mine now, permanently!

My crying colleague with whom I'd swapped went on to become the head of materials management in one year. I labored at being the best I could at my newly permanent job. I hired, trained, and challenged a new staff member to develop a new program for young professionals that ultimately gained popularity in our region, on local radio, and on Japanese radio and was featured in the state library journal. Later, she and I presented together at a state conference about our motivating and supportive relationship, the success of the program, and the ongoing services it sparked for the audience, such as book clubs at local bars.

Despite this success, I never regained favor or support in the organization. Over time, my early kudos and promise began to turn into negative feedback. I received a much lower appraisal in the next cycle and was forced to go to midlevel managers training—a step back from the leadership training I'd previously attended. I was blocked from attending training afforded to other managers at my level. In one instance, the head of county HR contacted me to say that a six-month cohort was available again, and she had one spot left after accommodating everyone, including those my director recommended for the class. She said it was the last time it would be offered in this form, and she could see no reason that I couldn't register. I told her that the library was different, and she should speak to my director, who previously had twice denied my attendance at this training. My direct supervisor informed me the next morning that my attendance at the training was being denied again for "business reasons." I simply couldn't be spared from my location for the two days per month over the six months scheduled for the training.

It seemed my fall from grace began to affect my branch and direct reports. Our decisions and shortcomings were met with heightened scrutiny. My subordinate supervisor was reprimanded directly from the director and labeled anti-LGBT for enforcing a rule regarding solicitation on library grounds that we'd always enforced the same way. A staff member leading a local author program was hospitalized, and I stepped in at the last minute to ensure the show went on. The author complained that the program had not met his expectations, and this showed up in my appraisal. When the time came for us to submit our renowned program for acceptance into the state conference, I realized it was best not to inform my direct supervisor or the director or we would likely be blocked. When a neighboring location's submission was accepted, it was celebrated in a system-wide memo. Our acceptance at that same conference was met with surprise, but we were happy there was no way for our superiors to block our work from statewide recognition—it was that dynamic!

THE TURNING POINT: EEO COMPLAINT FILING

Over time, I felt I needed to take action. Two more staff members who'd been acting heads of departments were permanently placed in system-wide "head of department" positions. By this time, the entire senior executive team of five had all been appointed without the positions being listed or recruited or interviews being held.

On graduation day from the midlevel managers cohort, the county executive spoke to my cohort and introduced the county's new focus on diversity and inclusion. Each department and agency in the county would be required to report on strategies to improve those elements in hiring at all levels. I later found the library's report on diversity and inclusion while perusing through system-wide files. The report indicated that all six members of the library's executive team were White females because there were no qualified minority librarians interested in department head positions due to the existence of a major library employer in a neighboring city that offered better work schedules. All department head positions became vacant during my tenure at the system, but the director had appointed someone to each position after a brief acting stint. One only lasted three days!

The report concluded that no Equal Employment Opportunity (EEO) complaints had ever been filed against the library. After years of feeling held back, with heightened scrutiny, lack of support, blocked training, and no opportunity to even apply for a promotion, this finding was the last straw for me. I'd heard from many that the system systematically held minorities back, but I felt I was extremely qualified, hardworking, and initially considered to be leadership material. I felt that I could be the one to speak out and win for all those who shared stories of maltreatment over the years. I called county human resources to file a formal complaint about it all.

The intake officer for the county was an African American man who listened intently to my story. He expressed surprise and concern. Based on my race, experiences, and the information from the EEO report I'd found, he recommended that I file an EEO report with the county for unfair hiring practices. Several months passed while I filed the official complaint documentation, defended it, and held the confidence during the process. An internal investigation was held. During the process, I was called to library HR for what my direct supervisor called an unprofessional e-mail I'd sent to her. The complaint could not be sustained in person when the head of HR read my e-mail aloud. I asked if this was the beginning of retaliatory harassment, and both feigned surprise. They had heard nothing about my formal EEO complaint.

Ultimately, my EEO complaint failed at the county level. The initial intake officer seemed pained to inform me that I had not prevailed. He strongly encouraged me to hire an attorney and take my case to the state or federal levels. Several of my mentors of various races had warned me not to file the complaint in the first place. Since I'd received another job offer at a nearby library system, I took my loss and left for new opportunities, putting the whole ordeal behind me.

For months and years afterward, colleagues I'd left behind shared internal messages about how new job openings were being handled. It often appeared that positions were now being opened to internal and external applicants. However, I and most others still felt the director was continuing to handpick from her favorites. The occasional minority would be brought in from the outside and given lower-level management status, but ultimately, they would have similar experiences and then leave. One was referred to me, and we shared similar stories once she told me she was leaving that system. I thought the experience was behind me; however, when I began applying for my next promotion, I was not able to get hired in any other system in that state, despite nurturing my growing network through professional associations.

One day a former colleague from that system contacted me and shared that she and several of her friends and colleagues (all African American librarians) had been contacted by a headhunter about an opening for a department head at that system. She and those in our network were pleasantly surprised to learn that this system would invest time and resources into their lip service on diversity and inclusion. I was stunned when my direct supervisor at my new system resigned, announcing that he had accepted a position as department head on the executive team in my previous library system. He was the first African American and male on that team during the 10 years I'd been affiliated with it.

While I'm happily enjoying a promotional opportunity in a new system in another state so many years later, I can't help but wonder what transpired to make this happen. What are the chances that this route would be taken after years of the director appointing all White women prior to my complaint?

How interesting that my direct supervisor ended up being hired by the organization that I formerly worked for.

CONTEMPLATING LESSONS LEARNED

In looking back on my ordeal with that system, I've wondered what I may have learned and whether I would still take the same actions if faced with that today. Would I have the courage and determination, especially realizing the toll I think it took on my career and my psyche? Instead of filing the complaint, could a conversation with my direct supervisor and the director have led to change? What might have happened if I had built a coalition with other coworkers who had similar complaints rather than going it completely alone? Perhaps I could have been more successful with additional voices and examples. Would I have prevailed had I taken my complaint to the state or federal EEO offices?

I doubt that the director ever reflected about my experience there and found any merit in my complaint. I'm even more doubtful that she would ever admit issues with her hiring practices—in reality or even in perception. I would like to think that my ill-fated complaint did help in the end when a headhunter was hired and diversity was eventually brought to their executive team. I hope this is just one step toward efforts to breathe reality into their oft-touted dedication to diversity and inclusion throughout the library and the county.

Chapter Sixteen

Disability and the Library Workplace

JJ Pionke

To strive, to seek, to find and not to yield.

—Alfred, Lord Tennyson

I got my start on disability and accessibility research and advocacy because the bathroom near my office went down for renovation in the spring of 2015. I am a person of size, and I work in a building dating back to 1926, when people were smaller vertically and horizontally. I asked five different people where I could use the bathroom, and I got five different answers. This started what I colloquially referred to as "The Great Bathroom Hunt." Using a map that the library gave out to patrons and visitors, I walked the entire building in search of the bathroom that would work best for me. As I walked, I found that the map was quite inaccurate, as new rooms were not listed. The map showed where bathrooms were spatially but not where the entrances were, which made it hard to actually find the bathrooms at times. Bathrooms had poor signage and were not marked as to whether there was an accessible toilet within.

I saw more problems as I walked the building, such as an interior ramp without a handrail, snow on the handicap ramps coming into the building, poor signage on how to find places within the library, and inaccurate wall maps that were decades out of date. With all of that, the library building that I work in is technically Americans With Disabilities Act (ADA) compliant. The ADA is a complex civil rights law that covers the accessibility of spaces, as well as discrimination in employment based on disability. The law contains many subparts that pertain to building codes, exceptions, and implementation. I would say that at the time of my walkthrough, the building was definitely not very accessible, but it was ADA compliant.

The library that I work in is like most libraries in general, especially those that inhabit older buildings. It's not that libraries and the people who work in them are deliberately out to be ableist but rather that there is a fundamental misunderstanding of what disability is and how to navigate accessibility. All of this is especially true for patrons as well as library employees with disabilities, and ADA covers both. Most libraries focus on physical disabilities and the accommodations for them, such as ramps, accessible bathrooms, and height-adjustable tables, but the ADA covers far more than that. The ADA was meant to cover all disabilities, encompassing sensory and mental, which includes autism, attention deficit disorder, and dyscalculia. The law is supportive of people with disabilities and makes allowances for accommodations, which are items or actions enabling people to operate efficiently and to effectively do their jobs. However, there can be resistance by library employees to ask for what they need and for libraries to honor those accommodation requests because of misunderstandings, miscommunication, and a lack of education.

The causes for employee hesitancy to ask for accommodations are rooted most often in stigma, especially if the disability is a mental illness. Stigma is associated with shame, and this ties directly into the American myth of rugged survival and success in the face of adversity. If you are asking for help because of a disability, then clearly you have already failed in life, or at least that might be what runs through your head when you ask for an accommodation. You may also feel that someone worse off might need what you're asking for. As a person with posttraumatic stress disorder (PTSD), I can certainly attest to the mixed feelings that can envelop us when we are going through the accommodations process. However, I would argue that we should be asking for what we need, even in the face of adversity, because we are all individuals with individual differences and individual needs.

Accommodation is ultimately about equity versus equality, but many people mistake these as being the same thing. Equality is everyone getting the same office supplies and office configurations, in the interest of fairness. Equity is actually giving people what they need to do their job well. For example, a standard-issue stapler is useless if you don't have the hand strength or hands to use it. The driving force behind equality is that we are all on the same level, but the actual reality is that we aren't. Our bodies, minds, and sensory organs are all different in some way. Some people are depressed, others have weakened immune systems, and there are always people with temporary disabilities from accidents. No one has a perfectly functioning body, and while most regular office configurations can adapt easily to a large range of variation, when the adaptation requires more than is typical, that is when it becomes an accommodation. Accommodations are not about equality. They are about equity so that there can be equality in the amount of work that is done.

THE ACCOMMODATION PROCESS

What does the accommodation process look like from the inside? For me, it was a bewildering, scary, and frustrating experience. The process really starts with acknowledging to yourself that you need help. Unfortunately, far too many of us wait until we are in a crisis to ask for help. This was certainly the case for me. The impact of all of the noise and hypervigilance because of where my office was located accumulated over time, until I was a nervous and very frustrated wreck. Once I admitted that I needed help, I started looking into the accommodation process. A person who doesn't have a diagnosis for their condition has to obtain one prior to requesting an accommodation.

The process seemed straightforward but involved a lot of waiting and anxiety for me. The short version involved reaching out to the accommodation specialist to talk about my disability and potential accommodations, providing the office with documentation and other paperwork, and then waiting for the accommodation specialist to negotiate on my behalf. Sometimes the accommodation process is quick, especially in cases where the accommodations are low or no cost. However, my accommodation was much more substantial, and there was significant pushback to the accommodations that were proposed.

The longer version of the accommodation process went like this: I disclosed my disability to my place of employment by disclosing my accommodation to an accommodation specialist. Then, I needed to get medical documentation about my condition. Initially, I was asked for a medical doctor's note, but I queried whether that was really needed from a doctor. While I do have a doctor for my health-care needs, he generally takes care of my medication and physical health. My therapist was the person who was actively treating my PTSD. What the accommodation specialist really wanted was a letter from the professional who was most actively treating me. After getting a letter from my therapist, the accommodation specialist and I had to discuss what accommodations would be best for the symptoms that I was experiencing. This involved, in part, looking into the Job Accommodation Network (JAN) database to see what recommendations there were for my condition and symptoms. Once that was done, the accommodation specialist presented a proposal to the library and negotiated the recommended accommodations on my behalf and in my absence, as I was not allowed to attend the meetings, per university policy.

The accommodation process is an iterative one, so I tried a lot of different accommodations to see what would and would not work. I remained dedicated to the process, but my frustration and anxiety levels grew as the time from my initial filing started to grow. After six months, I hired a lawyer who specializes in disability, and I also made the decision to go back on the job market and leave a job that I loved. Neither choice was an easy one to make, and going back on the job market was especially heartbreaking and caused me to become severely depressed. I hired a lawyer in part because I knew the law was on my side, and I wanted the process to come to a resolution because my mental health was suffering severely.

My rationale for returning to the job market revolved around the idea that, if my place of employment didn't value my health, which includes mental health, then what was the point in remaining? After fighting so hard to get assistance for my mental health, I was not going to let a job destroy the peace of mind that I had finally been getting through years of therapy. Once the lawyer got involved, the process moved more quickly. After nine months, I finally got the accommodations that I needed, but I had suffered a lot of anxiety and fear, many sleepless nights, and more tears than I care to think about.

It seemed that the accommodation process was a waiting game, which it was, and it took a serious toll on me. I often felt hurt because I thought I was a valued member of the library's team. Yet my request for the accommodations that I needed to not only survive but also thrive was being met with opposition. Though I was the person who needed the accommodation, I was generally excluded once I started the process. Everything was conducted through the accommodation specialist, and since I wasn't part of the discussions, I often felt I had no idea what was going on. The uncertainty and the waiting made my anxiety and PTSD much worse. No process is ever perfect, and improvements can always be made. Since my case, there have been changes in both the library and the university in regard to the accommodation process. The university hired more accommodations specialists, and the library reviewed policies and assigned an employee to work on disability accommodation more exclusively.

CONCLUSION

A question that I get from time to time is, what happened after "The Great Bathroom Hunt"? The short version is, I prepared a PowerPoint presentation that highlighted, with pictures, the problems that I had found. Backed up by student anecdotes, I went to a meeting with several people in authority and talked about my findings. As of this writing, most of the issues that were brought up in that meeting have been addressed. For example, the building was outfitted with uniform signage, both for wayfinding and for room numbering; a handrail was installed on an interior ramp that needed it; and the building maps that were distributed to patrons and visitors were redone to improve readability. Reaction from the library in terms of making it more accessible has been largely positive, with a few individuals lamenting,

"We've always done it this way." In general, it has been my experience that libraries want to better support patrons with disabilities, but many do not realize they are doing a poor job of meeting the needs of this group of patrons.

In regard to my accommodation, it's working out just fine. I'm much happier and far more productive because of the accommodation. However, the length, frustration, and anxiety of my accommodation took a toll on me. I am more cautious and less flexible in terms of any changes to my accommodation or work environment after having struggled so hard. There were also social consequences in terms of exclusion from events and other incidences. In general, however, I would argue that problems related to the accommodation process have more to do with not knowing or understanding what employees really need rather than outright ableist hostility (though at times that can be present). Accessibility for patrons and library employees alike has a long way to go. I believe we can get there with commitment to education and making changes at all levels.

ADDITIONAL READINGS

A to Z of disabilities and accommodations. Job Accommodation Network. Retrieved on October 19, 2018, from https://askjan.org/a-to-z.cfm

Library services for people with disabilities policy. Association of Specialized, Government, and Cooperative Library Agencies. Retrieved on October 19, 2018, from http://www.ala.org/asgcla/resources/libraryservices

Procedures for providing reasonable accommodation for individuals with disabilities. Equal Employment Opportunity Commission. Retrieved on October 19, 2018, from https://www.eeoc.gov/eeoc/internal/reasonable_accommodation.cfm

Chapter Seventeen

Say My Name

Transgender Acceptance Across Campus

Amy Kautzman and Beth Lesen

I am larger, better than I thought, I did not know I held so much goodness.
—Walt Whitman

This voice addresses how California State University, Sacramento (CSUS), made it a priority to build a culture of respect and inclusion for its transgender and gender-nonconforming students. It describes the ongoing work it takes to signal true acceptance and integration from the shared perspectives of student affairs and the university library. In reference to this chapter, the term *transgender* represents transgender, transitioning, gender-nonconforming, nonbinary, and more.

BUILDING A CORE CAMPUS TEAM

Sacramento State is a diverse campus committed to education equity and the creation of an inclusive campus. We are officially designated as both a Hispanic-serving institution (HSI) and an Asian-American Native American Pacific Islander serving institution (AANAPISI) with an enrollment of more than 30,000 students in California's capital city. Living our ideals takes substantial work that includes looking deeply at how the university supports its transgender and gender-nonconforming community.

Previously, caring campus staff and faculty members supported our transgender students in a piecemeal fashion, with the responsibility for finding the right resources falling on the student. There was no campus-wide structure by which students could be assured that their needs would be recognized and

149

consistently met across campus. This lack of standardized support caused unacceptable levels of stress for our students and put their timely graduation at risk, as the probability of dropping classes was very high when a student felt unsafe. In 2015, newly hired coauthor Amy Kautzman, university library dean and director, initiated the preferred-name (the name a person wishes to be known by) conversation at Sacramento State, as she had successfully led the effort at the University of California, Davis (UCD), to deploy an automated preferred-name process for all students. Kautzman saw that Sacramento State had the willingness and desire to implement a similar change.

To improve support for transgender students, it became obvious that the campus needed to create global policies and practices in support of a preferred-name process for our transitioning and gender-nonconforming students and to change restrooms to be gender inclusive. These top two priorities came directly from student feedback, where they shared their anxiety about being outed without their permission during routine interactions with staff and faculty members on campus and when they could not readily locate gender-inclusive restrooms.

With the goal of fully supporting our transgender students' preferred-name choices and enabling access to an equitable number of gender-inclusive restrooms, Kautzman and Beth Lesen, Sacramento State's associate vice president and dean of students, worked to transform the Sacramento State experience for transgender students. For any university to enable a "preferred-name process," it is imperative that campus leadership explicitly supports the goal of honoring the experiences of transgender students and faculty on campus by committing hundreds of staff hours toward what is commonly an unfunded mandate. At Sacramento State, we recruited a team of people representing the library, student affairs, facilities, campus counsel, enrollment management, registrar's office, campus life, academic affairs, faculty senate, Office of Equal Opportunity, human resources, university communications, information resources and technology, campus PRIDE center, health and counseling, athletics, and students. The team was initially broken into three subgroups: a steering committee consisting mainly of administrators; a working group consisting of administrators, staff, and faculty; and a small student advisory group. The teams were charged with identifying the specific problems the project would address and which staff members would be assigned to each. There were four issues to be addressed: dataflow, policy limitations, accessibility of facilities, and training needs. Our experience will guide readers on how they can begin the conversation on their own campus.

LEGAL NAME TO PREFERRED NAME:
IT IS ALL ABOUT THE DATA

One's legal name is required for financial aid, payroll, transcripts, health services, and diplomas. The authoritative source that decides how a name will be used is the campus information system. The student's legal name is fed into the campus information system and used for registration, grading, transcripts, and building student rosters. These systems are large and complex and often decades old, with many layers of updates. Changing the coding, literally hacking the system, often causes unintended problems, and because of these unforeseen side effects, most campuses are reluctant to make changes that could affect system stability. The campus information system also supplies the data (name) to multiple secondary systems, which do not require legal names and can serve up preferred names. Examples of these secondary systems include class rosters, ID cards, e-mail, and campus directories, among others. An inclusive campus endeavors to make the preferred name the default in the maximum number of feasible areas, only using the legal name where there exists a clear and required need. Ideally, when legal names are necessary, the preferred name would also be noted, and staff privy to that information would be trained to interact appropriately and respectfully.

The student name that goes into the system serves as "the name" that is transferred to all other connected systems across campus. Therefore, any conversation about privileging a preferred name, gender, and pronoun must begin with the registrar's office (which provides the name) and the IT group (that supports the student information system). Fortunately, many campuses have successfully implemented preferred-name practices, and there is a growing number of system administrators who can lend their experience in resolving the dataflow problem. Even with this help, personalizing how names are used in a local system is never simple. The campus information system is built on proprietary software; hacking the code is difficult and may void the campus contract.

In 2017, EDUCAUSE formed a working group to address the demands of the May 2016 Department of Education "Dear Colleague Letter on Transgender Students" (Lhamon & Gupta, 2016) that reiterates how Title IX protects all students from sex discrimination. In April 2018, the EDUCAUSE group published a report (Borgione et al., 2018) that directly addresses the need for student information systems to incorporate gender identities, pronouns, and preferred names of students, faculties, and staffs. In the future there will be an out-of-the-box solution, but for now we need to work within our legacy systems. Changing the way a name flows through any information system is difficult, and because of the inherent risk, disrupting the distribution of standard information is seldom attempted. The stakes are high if a database error happens and a student's, staff member's, or faculty member's birth name or gender is outed as a result of a dirty dataflow. Another issue can be the problem of personnel who may not always respect the sanctity of the student's privacy. The first problem can be abolished with coding; the second, with training and an emphasis on building a culture of respect.

THE DATA ARE WRANGLED; WHAT NOW?

It is a huge success to decipher the coding and replace the legal with the preferred name. The next step is for the campus to decide on and codify the process by which a student may request a preferred name and how the name change is put into effect. It is at this point in the project where the emphasis moves from computer science to workflows and information security. On most campuses, only the first name is allowed to be changed, but some campuses also allow the surname to be changed. Concerns around changing first and last names (testing center access and other scenarios where a name or photo verification is required) are alleviated when the ID card is updated with the new name. In effect, the ID number, not the name, becomes the primary identifier. Finally, the campus also needs to ascertain who will have access to the files with the legal name and how to train units to retain privacy regarding students, faculty members, and staff members who have transitioned.

Once rules are set and a process has been established, the workflow and policy need to move from theory to practice. We strongly suggest that a pilot is put into place with students who are willing to live with the fact that their data may be exposed in a manner that is not optimal. At this stage of the project, the team needs a real example, and this person should be expected to

- Change their name through an automated or mediated system
- Change e-mail if the name is based on legal first name
- Pick up a new ID card with the preferred name
- See their preferred name on a class rosters, library e-mails, campus directory, and other common forms of campus communication

GOING LIVE

Once the system is tested and proves to be robust enough to go live, then it is time to develop a "go-live" plan. Working with campus communications, it is optimal to craft a public announcement and build a web presence (generally on the campus registrar's site) that explains the purpose and limitations of the preferred-name process. In reality, there will be cisgender staff members who will actively work against policy and procedure changes that support our transgender students. This is why it is necessary to have explicit support and training from university leadership at the beginning of this project. It is also the primary reason access to legal names and gender markers should be limited to those whose work requires the data. Staff and faculty members should be trained in confidentiality best practices and supported by training not unlike the expectations for the Family Educational Rights and Privacy Act (FERPA).

Training, such as Safe Space/Safe Zone (https://thesafezoneproject.com) helps preferred-name implementers and colleagues understand where they fall in the continuum from bias to acceptance and how, as an ally, they can better support their community. Opposition to people outside of the gender binary (beyond male/female) comes not only from critics but also from transgender allies who are not aware of how the institutional structures they built and work within carry out everyday acts of bias.

GENDER-INCLUSIVE RESTROOMS

In 2015, the U.S. Transgender Survey (USTS) questioned 28,000 respondents about their lives. This was the largest survey to date that captured the transgender experience, and the results showed that the lack of access to safe restrooms had detrimental effects on the respondents' lives. According to the data (James et al., 2016),

- More than half (59%) of the respondents avoided using a public restroom in the past year because they were afraid of confrontations or other problems they might experience.
- Nearly one third (32%) of the respondents limited the amount that they ate and drank to avoid using the restroom in the past year.
- Eight percent (8%) reported having a urinary tract infection, kidney infection, or another kidney-related problem in the past year as a result of avoiding restrooms.

The survey shows the necessity of accessible and appropriate restrooms, but change is neither simple nor inexpensive. There are federal, state, and local codes regulating the number of available toilets per number of employees. It is very easy to change single-stall restrooms from single-sex to gender-inclusive toilets. For those of us with multiple stall rooms, we need to be more persistent and creative. Part of the solution is acknowledging that our transgender campus community members are not the only people with needs that are not supported by the group-toilet approach. Parents with opposite-sex children, health aids with disabled clients, and our friends with catheters or other health needs also desire single-person restrooms. By presenting a myriad of audiences with specific restroom needs, we can make a comprehensive argument for change that provides underserved patrons dignified restroom options and also provides some political cover in states where bathroom politics have become a proxy for all things gender-scary.

At Sacramento State the dual focus has been on advocating for gender-inclusive restrooms in new construction and implementing Assembly Bill 1732, a bill requiring that all single-stall restrooms in the state of California be designated "gender neutral." Additionally, there is an active movement toward designating select multistall restrooms as gender-inclusive restrooms. While this may require conversations across units, it can be easily accomplished and is supported by the California State University Technical Bulletin (Kennedy, 2017). The health and wellness facility on campus includes five gender-inclusive restrooms as do other buildings that occupy central locations on this 300-plus-acre campus. Geography is important with respect to access with newer buildings and remodels offering the opportunity to implement changes.

Planning Priorities for Limited Bathroom Resources

- Create a list of bathroom options currently available in all buildings.
- Build a web page with maps that list and illustrate family, ADA, and gender-inclusive restrooms, as well as spaces for nursing mothers and those with child changing tables.
- Consider adding your bathroom options to the Refuge Restrooms site (https://www.refugerestrooms.org), which provides a list of safe restroom access across the United States.

CAMPUS LIFE

Involved and engaged students tend to be more successful. However, a substantial amount of campus life is segregated by binary gender. Historically, new students are assigned to rooms in residence halls based on gender. Sports (including intramurals and sport clubs, as well as NCAA) are segregated by gender. A few years ago, the California State University (CSU) system Executive Order 969 (Reed, 2006) mandated that all student clubs must be open to all students without restriction. Therefore, gendered clubs may have a gender in their title, but they must be open to any potential new member on campus. This is one example of how the campuses that have chosen to do this work actively and early are creating positive change across campuses.

Room assignments for new students—a historically gender-segregated setup—is more nuanced. The interests of all students need to be balanced. To address potential housing issues, a checkbox was included on the housing application that indicated openness to gender-inclusive housing arrangements. Students who checked that box effectively self-identified as being willing to live with gender-nonconforming students. There was also a statement indicating that accommodations are made on an individual basis with a space available to indicate the need for trans-inclusive housing. Transgender students reach out to be assured that their gender identity will be accepted and they will feel safe and welcomed. When this happens, housing staff pull from that identified group of students for their roommate assignments. In this way there is some assurance that incoming transgender students will be welcomed by their roommates.

At a minimum, campus life staff should be safe-zone trained, in addition to participating in diversity training to equip them with information necessary to work well with a variety of students. Moments when students are seeking medical or counseling assistance are typically vulnerable times, so it's especially important for staff members delivering those services to be sensitive to the needs of transgender students, so they can respond in the best possible ways. Otherwise transgender students will be understandably reluctant to access services that may be critical to their success and well-being. It is a good idea to offer some of the staff additional, intensive training on working with transgender students in ways that are specific to their disciplines. For example, our medical and psychological staff in Student Health and Counseling Services is periodically trained by staff from Sacramento's Gender Health Center. Because transgender students tend as a group to experience higher rates of depression and suicidal ideation, it's particularly important that Student Health and Counseling is an area where they feel welcomed and safe.

CONTINUING THE WORK

The best way to ensure that the work of inclusion seeps into all aspects of campus life is to train the various content experts well and then empower them to audit their own areas, holding them accountable for identifying and implementing specific changes. This was how Sacramento State's career center noticed that an atypical gender presentation may become a barrier in a student's job search. This led to the career center staff conducting a small focus group to determine what needs they may not have been meeting for transgendered job seekers. Now programming is offered to discuss a variety of issues, including gender identity and presentation in the job search, as well as how to decide whether, what, and when to disclose. Articulating trans-inclusiveness as a priority, equipping people across campus with the information and understanding they need, and then creating an expectation and a process of accountability ensures that the work of trans-inclusiveness stays on the radar and is dynamic rather than a static process.

One amazingly positive outcome that came out of the work at UCD and CSUS is expanded training and policy from the campus police departments. In fact, the UCDPD was the first university police department to write a campus policy on community preferred names (UC Davis Police Department, 2018). Based on UCD's excellent work, the CSUSPD also developed their own policy, which ensures that, when the police interact with transgendered community members, they have undergone some training, and the expectations of respect and process have been codified.

When you choose to engage in social justice work on campus, you will quickly find out that the work is complicated, political, and accomplished by dozens of good people who have invested their passion and expertise to effect change on their campus. None of this work could have happened without the patience and generosity of transgender people who took time out of their studies to actively inform the process along the way. To experience the best success, having an advisory group of people who have this lived experience is critical, and as with so many things, when in doubt, ask.

REFERENCES

Assem. Bill 1732, 2015–2016, Chapter 818, 2016 Cal. Stat. Retrieved from https://leginfo.legislature.ca.gov/faces/billVersionsCompareClient.xhtml?bill_id=201520160AB1732

Borgione, L., Elliott, J., Hahn, S., Hart, M., Jetto, E., Koralesky, B., . . . Wells, E. (2018). Gender identity in higher education: Recommendations for campus information systems. Retrieved from https://library.educause.edu/resources/2018/4/gender-identity-in-higher-education

James, S., Herman, J., Rankin, S., Keisling, M., Mottet, L., & Anafi, M. (2016). The report of the 2015 U.S. transgender survey. Washington, DC: National Center for Transgender Equality. Retrieved from https://transequality.org/sites/default/files/docs/usts/USTS-Full-Report-Dec17.pdf

Kennedy, T. (2017). Inclusion of all-gender multi compartment toilet room facilities in CSU facilities [CPDC—A/E Technical Bulletin]. California State University Office of the Chancellor. Retrieved from http://www.calstate.edu/CPDC/AE/memos/TB-17-004_all-gender_inclusion.pdf

Lhamon, C., & Gupta, V. (2016). Dear colleague letter on transgender students. Letter prepared for U.S. Department of Justice, Civil Rights Division/U.S. Department of Education, Office for Civil Rights. Retrieved December 3, 2018, from https://www2.ed.gov/ocr/letters/colleague-201702-title-ix.pdf

Reed, C. (2006). Student activities—Executive Order No. 969 [Memorandum]. California State University Office of the Chancellor. Retrieved from https://www.calstate.edu/eo/EO-969.pdf

UC Davis Police Department. (2018). Community preferred names, policy 369. In *University of California Davis PD policy manual*. Retrieved from https://police.ucdavis.edu/sites/g/files/dgvnsk3476/files/inline-files/UC%20Davis%20Police%20Department%20Policy%20Manual_0.pdf

ADDITIONAL READINGS

Halberstam, J. (2018). *Trans*: A quick and quirky account of gender variability*. Oakland: University of California Press.

Mock, J. (2014). *Redefining realness: My path to womanhood, identity, love and so much more*. New York: Atria Books.

Nutt, A. E. (2015). *Becoming Nicole: The transformation of an American family*. New York: Random House.

Stryker, S. (2008). *Transgender history*. Berkeley, CA: Seal Press.

Chapter Eighteen

"Me, an Academic Librarian—Never"

*How the Knowledge River Program Paved the
Way for a Career in the Profession*

Gina Macaluso and Annabelle V. Nuñez

> We cannot teach people anything, we can only help them discover it within
> themselves.
>
> —Galileo Galilei

This chapter outlines the experience of a former Knowledge River (KR) Program scholar who charily applied for her first academic position at the University of Arizona Health Sciences Library (UAHSL) and later became an associate director for the library. Described from a personal lens, it charts a career path highlighting the features that make up the KR Program. This voice should speak to a range of people in the profession—from library and information science (LIS) program deans, directors, instructors, and students to library administrators who support workforce development through diversity and inclusion initiatives.

THE PROSPECT

For the daughter of immigrant parents, work was a priority over the pursuit of higher education. Thankfully, after high school my parents supported me enough to make it possible for me to attend the local junior college full time while holding down a part-time job. I was both excited and nervous at the same time as I was entering a new phase in my life that was full of unknowns. I did not know what to expect. There was no advanced education in my family history. A low score on the college entrance exam was the first time I questioned my ability to succeed in academia. I spent the first of three years in junior college taking remedial classes. I persisted and managed academically to successfully transfer to the University of Arizona. It was there I learned about student tracking in education. I realized that I had been that student. My high school advisor encouraged me to take such classes as home economics and typing. Never did we have a conversation about STEM (science, technology, engineering, and mathematics)–related courses, let alone my attending college.

The cards were stacked against me by all accounts. I was a first-generation college student from a low-income household lacking any kind of college readiness. Working through the barriers, I earned my undergraduate degree in theater education after six years. For more than a decade I worked for a local school district and then two nonprofit arts organizations. The work was rewarding; however, too many years of soft money funding had me longing for a master's degree. I wanted a career.

Despite earning my bachelor's degree—and not to minimize that achievement—the collegiate experience made a graduate education seem like a lofty and impossible goal. That narrative ran deep in my psyche, and just like that, graduate school would be just a dream, until . . .

LIBRARY SCHOOL

In 2003, I earned my library degree from the School of Information at the University of Arizona. I was in the first cohort of the inaugural class of the Knowledge River (KR) Scholars Program. The program began in 2001, funded substantially by the Institute of Museum and Library Services (IMLS). Knowledge River charted new territory in programs for addressing diversity in LIS education. Knowledge River "specializes in educating information professionals who have experience with and are committed to the information needs of Latino and Native American populations" (University of Arizona College of Social and Behavioral Sciences School of Information, n.d.). Knowledge River joins a small group of LIS programs that demonstrate the positive impact their respective diversity initiatives offer to transform the workforce and profession (Al-Qallaf & Mika, 2013).

Under the direction of coauthor Gina Macaluso, KR's 17th cohort, though slightly modified in 2018, still offers financial support that includes a graduate assistantship for work experience, opportunities for professional development, mentorship, custom advising, and the support of peer learners matriculating as a group. For me, a nontraditional student, these were the primary characteristics that factored into my decision to enroll.

THE STUDENT

For a year, I worked 20 hours a week as a graduate assistant with Patricia Tarin, the first Knowledge River program manager (2001–2007). I was one of three assistants who helped launch the program with 27 students in the first cohort. For one semester, I was a teaching assistant for the course entitled Issues in Information Resources from a Hispanic and Native American Perspective. It was the first elective course tailored in cultural pedagogy, creating a community of learners who supported retention and mitigated attrition (Angelino, Williams, & Natvig, 2007). The program established several elective courses based on the cultural pedagogy and cross-listed several courses from departmental programs, like Mexican American studies and American Indian studies.

Drawing upon previous work experience, I also helped Tarin develop a comprehensive orientation program to develop and establish our cohort bond and prepare the group for the rigors of graduate school. I helped expand the recruitment strategy by marketing the KR Program to targeted constituencies, such as professional associations in the LIS field like the American Indian Library Association (AILA) and REFORMA: The National Association to Promote Library and Information Services to Latinos and the Spanish-Speaking. We also targeted library schools and promoted the program opportunity on LIS LISTSERVs. Examples included the Public Library Association and key undergraduate cultural studies programs in academia, such as the Mexican American and American Indian studies programs at the University of Arizona. I had a lot of individual contact with prospective students working "to convince applicants of the benefits of a career in librarianship and the unique contributions they can make profession" (Montiel-Overall & Littletree, 2010). After several personal communications about KR, I would like to think I had a hand in successfully recruiting Mark Puente, director of diversity and leadership programs for the Association of Research Libraries, to the program. In my final semester, I worked as an administrative assistant to the director of the public library system. There I was also able to carve out time to work on the reference desk to gain experience working at the library's service point. Without the cohort experience, I would have struggled substantially, and that is why it is very important for me to pay it forward in my professional and administrative capacity.

THE COHORT MODEL

Today all new KR students take a foundational course together, Foundations of Library and Information Services, which provides an introduction to the information needs of the two targeted cultural communities. Because many of the courses are now online, this additional course gives students a chance to get to know each other and begin building relationships that often last beyond the semester. In addition to customized advisory support and a suite of courses based in cultural pedagogy, major national figures have been recruited to serve as adjunct faculty and guest lecturers. They include Elizabeth Martinez, Luis Herrera, Richard Chabran, Camila Alire, José Aponte, Marty de Montano, Loriene Roy, Cheryl Metoyer, and Hartman H. Lomawaima, to name a few. Networking with these and other library leaders in the profession opened a few doors for a number of KRs throughout the years.

WORK EXPERIENCE

After graduation I accepted a part-time position as a librarian at a public library. I enjoyed it because I was able to "serve my community," a common aspiration for many librarians of color. I was comfortable knowing I would easily slip into a full-time position once one became available.

The University of Arizona Health Sciences Library posted a new and unique position for the library. The job was a grant-funded, nontenure position for the Arizona Hispanic Center of Excellence (AHCOE). Toni Anaya, a former KR classmate and professional colleague, knew I was interested in health sciences. She nudged me to apply for the job, one I would have never considered applying for given my timid relationship with academia. This example illustrates the benefits of the cohort model that builds a community dedicated to diversity and inclusion in the profession. It provides not only social support for students but also support for alumni as they begin to navigate their professional careers.

I emerged as the successful candidate for the AHCOE position and knew I had a lot to prove. In 2004, I was on a year-to-year contract as the AHCOE librarian. For three years my work focused on supporting Hispanic students, faculty, and researchers at the College of Medicine. Drawing on my previous experience in the nonprofit field, I worked to engage key stakeholders and expand the library's outreach efforts to engage the community in health literacy programming. I reached out to schools, organizations, agencies, associations, and groups focused on Hispanic health and health disparities. I was a link to the community that the university was aspiring to reach. It was imperative for me to demonstrate the benefit of having a permanent librarian focused on diversity and inclusion in the health sciences library.

In 2007, my position changed, and I was given the status of continuing-eligible (toward tenure), which was my chance for a permanent position. My role changed from serving the Arizona Hispanic Center of Excellence at the College of Medicine to becoming the embedded liaison librarian to the Mel and Enid Zuckerman College of Public Health. I maintained my relationship with the KR Program by mentoring six KR students each year and by comanaging WE Search (2006–2009), a high school peer-to-peer library and health literacy program. Our outreach librarian, Pat Auflick, and I mentored KR scholars interested in health sciences librarianship. In subsequent years, I continued to mentor KR students interested in health sciences librarianship. The following quote is from Allison Herrera, cohort 15:

> The Knowledge River Scholar program gave me wonderful professional opportunities in Arizona that prepared me for my current position at the Harvard Medical School, Countway Library as a User Experience Researcher. I believe that gaining hands-on experience is invaluable for any professional who wants to work in libraries. At the University of Arizona Health Sciences Library, I worked with bright professionals with diverse backgrounds who supported and mentored me. (A. Herrera, personal communication, April 24, 2018)

PARTNERSHIPS FOR SUSTAINABILITY

The program has matured on campus, as evidenced by its increasing level of sustainability and institutional recognition, including the KR manager's position gaining faculty status. Funding from partnerships has grown over the years to support students via graduate assistantships, grants, internships, tuition discounts, and waivers. To date, the partners are the University of Arizona Libraries—Special Collections, Main Library, iSpace, and the Health Sciences Library; the university's Laboratory of Tree-Ring Research; the Arizona State Museum; the Pima County Public Library System; and the Arizona State University Libraries. KR's success at recruiting, matriculating, mentoring, advising, and graduating students in the program has resulted in an approximate 94.9% graduation rate. As of fall 2017, KR has supported more than 225 students. With the graduation of these students, KR will have placed more than 225 library professionals in the field who have demonstrated a commitment to serve the information needs of Latinos and Native Americans. Since 2006, I have served as a member of the KR advisory board and a KR mentor and have assisted with recruitment and programming. Now as the associate director of UAHSL, I work to procure funding from the National Library of Medicine to annually host a KR scholar, as well as oversee the graduate assistantship program for UAHSL. It is very gratifying to see former KR scholars at professional meetings, not only to catch up, but also to see them present their work as librarians.

RACIAL BREAKDOWN OF KR SCHOLARS

KR Scholars

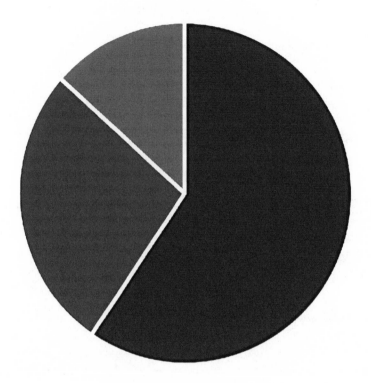

■ LatinX   ■ Native American   ■ Other

Figure 18.1.   Approximately 66 Native Americans, 134 Latinxs, and 25 others.

KR Scholars
Types of Employment

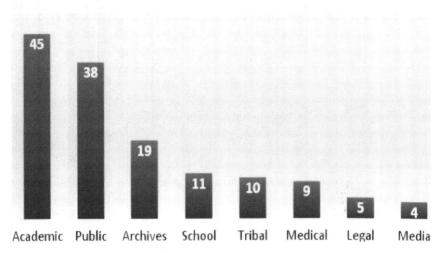

Figure 18.2. **KR Scholars work in all types of information organizations, including public, academic, medical, legal, special, tribal, and school libraries; historical societies; archives; and museums.**

CONCLUSION

The KR Program's unshakable foundation puts it in a position for expanding its national impact on libraries, their professional staff, and the communities they serve through the online program. By placing students at the center of learning and engaging them as creators, problem solvers, and potential leaders, KR has prepared them to provide culturally relevant, innovative, and effective service in information environments that anchor their local and global communities. KR is successful because of the work experience that comes from the extended community of support, the partners, and those who serve as role models, mentors, and advisors. Recruitment and retention of students goes much further than just offering financial assistance.

KR scholars have a profound impact across the nation, as well as in Mexico, Canada, and Australia. In addition to the geographical areas in which KR scholars are making a difference, 13 scholars have a PhD or have gone into doctoral programs, thereby adding to the depth of library research. Sure, students have expressed gratitude for the financial support they've received through the program. But when you get to know their stories and their backgrounds, it is evident that there is much more going on than just the funding. KR offers a holistic approach to success in graduate school.

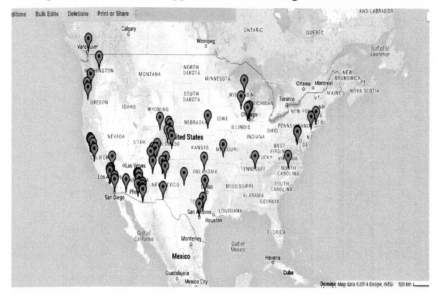

Figure 18.3. Snapshot of where KR scholars are making a difference in their communities.

REFERENCES

Al-Qallaf, C., & Mika, J. (2013). The role of multiculturalism and diversity in library and information science: LIS education and the job market. *Libri, 63*(1), 1–20. doi:10.1515/libri-2013-0001

Angelino, L. M., Williams, F. K., & Natvig, D. (2007). Strategies to engage online students and reduce attrition rates. *Journal of Educators Online, 4*(2). doi:10.9743/jeo.2007.2.4

Montiel-Overall, P., & Littletree, S. (2010). Knowledge River: A case study of a library and information science program focusing on Latino and Native American perspectives. *Library Trends, 59*(1), 67–87.

University of Arizona College of Social and Behavioral Sciences School of Information. (n.d.). Knowledge River. Retrieved from https://ischool.arizona.edu/knowledge-river-0

Chapter Nineteen

Creating a Successful Task Group on Diversity

Brenda Linares and Ene Belleh

We need to give each other the space to grow, to be ourselves, to exercise our diversity. We need to give each other space so that we may both give and receive such beautiful things as ideas, openness, dignity, joy, healing, and inclusion.

—Max De Pree

Diversity is important, not just for institutions, but also for organizations. As people of color, it helps to see ourselves being represented in both the membership and the leadership of the organizations of which we are members. When it comes to medical librarianship, the representation of people of color still needs a lot of work. Therefore, it is important to have organizations that support professional goals and create welcoming environments to network with others.

In 2015, the Mid-Atlantic Chapter of the Medical Library Association (MAC/MLA) created the Diversity Task Group, the first of its kind among the MLA chapters. As pioneers in this effort, we highlight in this chapter our experience with establishing the group, discuss the group's progress, and share future plans now that the group has been promoted to a committee as of 2018. In outlining lessons learned and feedback from our members, we hope to assist other organizations that wish to undertake diversity-related efforts. As two of the current members of the MAC Diversity Task Group, we bring our perspectives on what we experienced. We share what we believed worked, lessons learned, challenges, and what should be considered when creating a diversity committee.

IT STARTED WITH LEADERS DESIRING A CHANGE IN THE ORGANIZATION

(*Brenda Linares*) As an American Library Association (ALA) Spectrum scholar and a Latina medical librarian, I know how important it is to have representation in an organization so that you feel welcome, supported, and accepted. I had been an active member of MAC/MLA for three years when I received a call from Ryan Harris, who was the Mid-Atlantic Chapter chair at that time. He shared that the executive board had proposed and approved the creation of a diversity task group, and he wanted me to be the chair. This new diversity task group would have two aims:

- Investigate ways MAC can promote diversity within the profession of medical librarianship
- Investigate ways MAC can encourage, develop, and promote diversity within MAC membership

I was surprised and excited about this opportunity, as it would be my first time overseeing a group like this. After searching for information about diversity-related task forces or committees in MLA and other regional chapters, I found out that this would be the first group of its kind. It certainly came as a surprise that this was the first time a regional chapter had created such a task group and that MLA chapters had not created diversity-related groups within the organization previously. Knowing that this type of work was important and dear to my heart, I accepted the appointment and looked forward to the opportunity.

MAC DIVERSITY TASK GROUP

Once I was appointed chair of the committee, the group was ready to get to work. There were six members in the task group from four different states (Maryland, North Carolina, Virginia, and Pennsylvania). We had two broad aims for the group and a very open timeline to accomplish our task. This provided us with a free-range approach of thinking about what we had to do and how long we had to do it. But it also created a challenging situation, since the aims were very broad, and we did not know where to start and what diversity topic to focus on first. We did not want to take too long to create an action plan and begin to get things done because we did not want to lose momentum. Therefore, we decided that the first thing we needed to do was to develop a definition of *diversity*. The concept of diversity needed to be inclusive, and we knew we could not just focus exclusively on one group or one diversity topic.

DECIDING ON A DEFINITION OF *DIVERSITY*

Defining *diversity* can be challenging and depends on what the intended focus of the group is. The focus could be solving a problem, addressing a need, or tackling a challenge. We spent quite a bit of time on this as we struggled to identify our focus. Group members did a lot of brainstorming, and several meetings were scheduled to discuss each members' findings. We bounced back and forth for a couple of weeks before settling on an adopted definition:

> We define *workforce diversity* as a collection of individual attributes that together help agencies pursue organizational objectives efficiently and effectively. These include, but are not limited to, characteristics such as national origin, language, race, color, disability, ethnicity, gender, age, religion, sexual orientation, gender identity, socioeconomic status, veteran status, and family structure. The concept also encompasses differences among people concerning where they are from and where they had lived and their differences in thoughts and life experiences.

TAKING ACTION: OUR NEXT STEP

As a group we also realized that diversity is a topic that could be mentioned or discussed briefly by people but then forgotten. We wanted to make sure something was done and that whatever came out of this group would be actionable items and things that could show results and effect change. We often hear people doing a lot of talking about the importance of diversity, but not much action is done. By the same token, no one wants to do anything that makes people uncomfortable. Our plan was to make sure we could come up with an action plan and something doable that would make a difference in our organization.

The group decided to conduct a short survey of MAC's membership composition to get baseline data and information to work with. In 2015, the six-question survey was sent to all current MAC members, and participation was voluntary. The questions included type of library work setting, the state where they were from, involvement with MAC, years of library work experience, ethnicity/race, and additional comments. We received a 42% response rate, with members offering additional comments and feedback.

Comments and Feedback From the Survey

- "Glad you are collecting data on this! Hope you get lots of responses."
- "Thanks to the MAC Diversity Task Group for taking this important project."

- "Are gender and LGBTQ status not areas of interest for MAC's diversity initiative?"
- "You should also have . . . asked about gender and LGBTQ to get a true picture of diversity."

WHAT WE ACCOMPLISHED

Since the first survey was only six questions, with a primary focus on collecting ethnic/racial demographics, we created a more extended version of the survey than had been planned from the beginning. We sought advice from diversity experts and people who do research on this topic and created a survey with 27 questions that were more inclusive and would provide additional information. This new, longer survey included questions on gender identity, gender, sexual orientation, language, race, ethnicity, years in the profession, years before retiring, and other questions designed to provide a clear picture of the membership composition of MAC. The survey was submitted through an Institutional Review Board process to be able to publish our findings.

The second survey was implemented in the summer of 2017 and yielded a 39% response rate. We planned to use the rich data that was collected to help us make recommendations and create a plan of action. The task group shared this preliminary data at the MAC Annual Conference in October 2017. We wanted to hear more from our members as part of this program, so we divided the audience into groups with some discussion questions. At the end of these discussions, we collected their written feedback and made it part of our data to analyze. While we were reviewing this data, we noticed that our membership felt they needed more information, training, and understanding of diversity issues, including awareness of implicit bias and microaggressions. Therefore, we decided to organize a program on implicit bias for the MAC 2018 annual conference. The program included a speaker who conducted an interactive session to get the audience involved and included in the conversation.

For our diversity task group efforts, we are also very proud as a chapter to have received the MLA Chapter Project of the Year Award at the MLA annual meeting in May 2018.

WHAT WORKED

Upon reflection of the first three years of MAC's work on diversity-related issues, we offer a compilation of the following processes and activities that the task group implemented:

- Created an inclusive definition of *diversity*.
- Implemented two surveys to get to know our membership and their priorities, so they could be part of the conversation.
- Made sure there was good communication among the group chair, group membership, and the organization membership.
- Promoted an open working environment for group members to express their opinions and ideas on what we needed to do to accomplish our goals.
- Enhanced accountability, with each member being committed and staying on schedule for all meetings. Members were mindful of deadlines, always met them, and delivered on what they were responsible for.
- Provided an opportunity for more ideas to be brought to the table and shared due to the diverse representation of the task group. Our ability to share ideas led to the success of the project, because everyone could offer different perspectives, contribute pros and cons, and suggest methods for accomplishing our goals.
- Communicated very effectively through e-mail and Zoom, which was essential since we were spread out in different states. The task group chair often sent out e-mails to set up meeting times via Doodle. Zoom allowed us to see documents so we could discuss them at the same time.
- Used Google Docs for managing, disseminating, and sharing information. Task group members could access meeting minutes and review survey questions and other data on their own time schedules.
- Set deadlines to help pull everything together and get information sorted in a timely manner.

We hope this reflective compilation assists other organizations interested in taking on this important work and creating diversity-related task groups and committees.

THINGS TO CONSIDER AND LESSONS LEARNED

Creating a successful diversity task group may not be an easy task, with everyone so busy with his or her own responsibilities. The key is to have members who care about the topic and will participate and help with the tasks of the group. The following aspects are important to consider when developing a diversity task group, task force, or committee:

- Determine the time zone of the members.
- Consider the flexibility of members' time and commitment.
- Make sure your group has defined and achievable goals and objectives. If they are too broad, make sure you have a discussion on how to accomplish what you need to do, and prioritize.

- Convey the importance for all members to understand what needs to be done.
- Creating a working timeline is essential for the process. This helps to keep group members engaged and committed to the project.
- Delegating is very important so that all members of the group can contribute.
- If you decide to do a survey, make sure you consult with someone who has experience and expertise on the topic to provide guidance on effective survey construction.
- Sending survey links in e-mails is good, but send reminders because many members forget to complete them.
- Keep in mind that the topic of diversity has different interpretations for people and that some might be defensive while others will be enthusiastic about it.
- People change jobs, and therefore having updated information is important.
- Scheduling can be a pain, but once you know what the group needs to do, make sure you block time in advance for conference calls and establishing timelines. Try to schedule more than one meeting at a time in advance.
- Be aware of your target audience. Knowing whom you intend to reach and impact will help to clarify the direction of the group and what you hope to achieve. Having a clear target audience will also come in handy when deciding on survey questions.
- Be sure to protect the process by allowing individual opinions to be heard and not suppressed, ignored, or discouraged.
- Define your desired outcomes, and identify champions.
- Clearly articulate what the expected deliverables are.
- Once you have your action plan, make sure you discuss how to implement it or put it into practice. It takes a long time to implement change and see results, so be patient.
- Be prepared to hear from people who may be reluctant to prioritize about this topic, as it may not concern them. Do not give up. Find supporters, and don't stop the conversation.
- Have an evaluation plan, and ask yourself these questions: Are you on the right track? Do you need to regroup, start again, or change priorities? Are you meeting your goals and expectations? Are your expectations reasonable?

CHALLENGES

- The initial aims given to the task group were twofold, broad, and lacked agenda in terms of what we needed to immediately address. Promoting diversity within the profession of medical librarianship is a much different and larger issue than promoting diversity within the MAC membership.

- Though our first focus was on the MAC membership, deciding what aspects of "diversity" we wanted to address was challenging and led the group to perhaps take on too many aspects at once.
- We were concerned with the fact that we were originally appointed as a task group and whether we would be able to achieve our goals within the limited time period. This became less of an issue once we requested and received approval for the task group to become a committee, since it would be difficult otherwise to achieve the goals.
- The project stalled after gathering the survey results. We struggled a bit with the analysis and what to do with the information we gathered.
- Not clearly identifying next steps could slow the whole process down.
- Getting members' schedules to coincide is often challenging.

SETTING GOALS

The following goals may be appropriate for others undertaking diversity-related work within their organizations:

- Address the lack of mentorship for minority professionals.
- Identify clearer pathways for minorities to attain leadership positions.
- Focus on the recruitment of minorities into the profession.
- Be attentive to the lack of opportunity for minorities to excel in the profession like their White counterparts.

NOW AND THE FUTURE

Initial cursory feedback indicates that the implicit bias session that we sponsored at the 2018 MAC conference was a success and hopefully will further stimulate a conversation of diversity and inclusion in our organization. We will continue to review the survey data we gathered to establish an action plan that provides deliverables and measurable outcomes for our organization. We also expect to follow through on our plan to initiate oral sessions to capture personal experiences and stories from a diverse representation of our members.

With the formation of the MLA Diversity and Inclusion Task Force, we hope to able to contribute as a group to those efforts, as well. We see this engagement as just the beginning of more diversity conversations to come, not just for our chapter, but for other chapters of MLA, as well.

Starting this type of group may not be easy, but with dedicated, supportive members and a set of achievable goals, you can start this engagement in your organization.

Chapter Twenty

Recommendations for Achieving Cultural Humility and Critical Consciousness in Cross-Cultural Communications

Kenyon Railey

Our lives begin to end the day we become silent about things that matter.
—Martin Luther King Jr.

Cross-cultural communication has become an increasingly important corner-stone of medical practice. Regarding race and ethnicity, the U.S. population is changing dramatically, and by 2044, more than half of all Americans will likely belong to a minority group (U.S. Census Bureau, 2014).

Since health sciences librarians interact with students, faculty members, community members, and patients from multiple backgrounds and are essential in health care teaching and research environments, the Association of College and Research Libraries (ACRL) developed standards in 2012 to "emphasize the need and obligation to serve and advocate for racial and ethnically diverse constituencies" (American Library Association, 2012). Due to this standard and in an effort to expand scholarship, there has been an increased emphasis for library and health sciences practitioners to become attuned to best practices in creating optimal experiences for constituents from a variety of backgrounds, languages, and abilities.

This chapter endeavors to add to that body of work by first discussing cross-cultural education through a consideration of past and present approaches. This is followed by specific recommendations to facilitate professional development, cultural humility, and improved cross-cultural communication among health science librarians, medical learners, and academic medicine leaders.

PAST CONCEPTS IN CROSS-CULTURAL EDUCATION

Over the last few decades, a variety of disciplines have shaped the current understanding of cultural competency. *Cultural competency* evolved as a popular term in the 1990s, and though there are many definitions, it generally means to develop an understanding of the needs of a diverse population while also learning how to interact effectively with people from varied cultural backgrounds (Mestre, 2010).

In the medical sphere, two landmark reports by the Institute of Medicine were very influential in highlighting cultural competency as a means to improve communication and ultimately care quality: "Crossing the Quality Chasm: A New Health System for the 21st Century" (2001) and "Unequal Treatment: Confronting Racial and Ethnic Disparities in Health Care" (2002; Betancourt, 2006). Since then, instruction methods have evolved to include recommendations on attitudes and skill development (Betancourt, 2003).

Despite a growing body of literature in the last quarter-century, no broadly accepted definition of *cultural competency* emerged, which led to great variation in teaching methods and efficacy within academic medical settings. Without a standardized definition and nonconsensus on the most effective instructional approaches, the reality is that incorporation of this training has remained difficult and often deemed inadequate.

Cultural humility rather than competency evolved as a potential conceptual method to instructional design (Tervalon & Murray-Garcia, 1998), particularly due to the notion that *competency* itself suggests a static endpoint and an implication that mastery could be achieved. Achieving humility as a goal is a process in progressing through cycles of self-reflection and self-awareness and one less steeped in knowledge and skill acquisition (Murray-Garcia & Tervalon, 2017).

EVOLVING CONCEPTS

Critical consciousness, a concept that applies critical analysis to culture and societal influences on behavior, may be the next level of intervention needed in cultural competency instruction. The development of critical thinking is crucial to analyzing patient problems in medical care. Providers of all stripes must learn to synthesize a wide variety of data while simultaneously considering varied diagnoses to determine a treatment plan. Critical consciousness, as it relates to health, combines critical thinking and cultural competency. Thinking critically about culture allows the medical learner to analyze a variety of sources and inputs that ultimately contribute to each patient's lived experience and illness. This includes biology but also history, geography, psychology, and other factors. As described by Kumagai and Lypson (2009), critical consciousness is "stepping back to understand one's own assumptions, biases, and values, and a shifting of one's gaze from self to others and conditions of injustice in the world" (p. 783).

SPECIFIC RECOMMENDATIONS

What, then, should we do to move away from cultural "competency" toward humility and critical consciousness? The remainder of this chapter offers some recommendations based on a study of the evidence, as well as personal experiences instituting this content in a multidisciplinary academic medical center.

Consistency

Most would agree that repetition and self-study are keys to any meaningful retention. No matter the field, in the simplest terms, "practice makes perfect." Despite this knowledge, cultural training is often relegated to "one-off" presentations, isolated lectures, or afternoon training sessions in medical education settings. Since working toward cultural humility and critical consciousness is a lifelong process, consistency in teaching these topics involves infusing content throughout any learner's educational experience. The implications of insufficiently timed, poorly planned, and improperly resourced interventions are extensive.

Second, it matters who attends and how often. Top-level administers and educators benefit from this type of training. Their attendance also delivers a message to the community of stakeholders that this educational training is important (Kripalani, Bussey-Jones, Katz, & Genao, 2006). An administrator who is perceived as being satisfied with simply "checking a box" by having a multicultural potluck or an isolated educational session is sending a message that this information is optional and not important. It worsens when leadership does not participate. Those who attend by choice can potentially become disillusioned by a lack of buy-in from those who are perceived to need the training. Moreover, those who attend by force can become disappointed by feeling their time is being wasted. Either of these outcomes can have the unintended consequence of worsening the perception of importance within the larger departmental culture.

The training format can and should vary, ranging from lectures and workshops to self-reflection exercises and experiential community or culture-focused activities.

No matter what method of cultural humility training or intervention is used, it must be longitudinal and integrated.

Critically Examine Race

Many large medical and research-oriented academic health centers are generally within or in the proximity of communities containing significant numbers of historically marginalized and impoverished populations. Therefore, it becomes paramount that people within academic medical settings work toward understanding the complex interplays between race and health. As knowledge of the human genome and ancestry has deepened over the last 30 years, scientists and laypeople alike are recognizing that race is, and always has been, a social construct. Genetic studies reveal that differences are more likely higher among currently defined racial groups than they are between these groups (Tsai, Ucik, Baldwin, Hasslinger, & George, 2016).

Historically, medical learners have not been exposed to the extensive body of research reflecting that race and racial categories are socially constructed. Misconceptions regarding race remain prominent in medicine. Recent studies have shown that individuals with at least some medical training, including medical students and residents, have astonishingly and inappropriately false health beliefs that likely affect clinical decision making (Hoffman, Trawalter, Axt, & Oliver, 2016).

By evaluating how race was presented within first- and second-year preclinical lectures, researchers at one medical school suggest that the inclusion of race without context or justification actually reinforced existing stereotypes and misconceptions (Tsai et al., 2016). Authors highlight the problematic nature of curricular practices that suggested race was a biological category instead of a social one.

The concept of microaggressions, a term used to describe subtle expressions of racism, deserves special mention. In a landmark work focused on microaggressions in clinical practice, Sue et al. (2007) defines this concept as "brief and commonplace daily verbal, behavioral, and environmental indignities, whether intentional or unintentional, that communicate hostile, derogatory, or negative racial slights and insults to the target person or group" (p. 273). The authors mention that, by ignoring subtle racism, it could "remain invisible" and have deleterious consequences.

Outside of psychology, there is a paucity of literature in medical education settings on microaggressions, including a study in academic library literature worth noting. Seeking to address the gap in literature within library information sciences related to racism, Alabi (2015) investigated if academic librarians of color were experiencing microaggressions from their library colleagues and if White majority librarians observed these exchanges directly. Through an online survey of 139 participants, the author observes that minority participants did experience and observe racial microaggressions more often than nonminority participants and that some academic librarians of color dealt with microaggressions perpetuated by colleagues in the workplace. Furthermore, nonminority librarians were unlikely to report observing microaggressions.

Although race is not a uniquely American problem, it should be noted that the problem has a special history here, which warrants examination for any medical provider and educator working within the U.S. health care system. The specifics are beyond the scope of this chapter, but given that the social construct of race is rooted in both conscious and unconscious thinking within the American psyche, entering into discussions related to this content must be taken with extreme care and intentionality. When engaging in conversations about race, academic medical community members must prepare themselves through a thorough evaluation and study of such topics as resistance, guilt, and privilege while also being prepared to discuss apathy, ambivalence, anxiety, and even anger. In order to truly move toward critical consciousness, culturally adept stakeholders must consider these elements, as well as concepts of personally mediated racism, institutionalized racism, microaggressions, and discrimination.

Contemplation and Self-Reflection

As mentioned earlier, working toward cultural humility requires an experiential understanding and acceptance of the beliefs, values, and ethics of others. To achieve cultural humility, skills must be acquired and evolving knowledge incorporated, coupled with a strong component of continuous self-reflection. Though not a new concept in medical education settings, self-reflection is an underutilized one. By facilitating a recognition of one's own views of the world, culture, bias, and even social justice, it could move us toward critical consciousness and how our views can affect interactions with others (Bullon, 2013). Narrative writing has also been suggested as a way to help trainees reflect on values and beliefs and potentially could be used in the successful implementation of cultural competency training (Kripalani et al., 2006).

There is movement of note in library sciences that incorporates self-reflective practices, notably involving social justice principles. Authors of one article evaluating lesbian, gay, bisexual, trans, and queer (LGBTQ) health in librarianship suggest that using reflective practices regarding sexuality and gender could ultimately shape one's approach when working with different populations (Hawkins, Morris, Nguyen, Siegel, & Vardell, 2017).

Contact and Empathy

Connection is at the core of establishing critical consciousness. This connection comes not only from self-reflection but also from studying issues of social justice, inequity, and cultural determinants of health.

As outlined in this chapter and others in this text, we live and learn in an increasingly diverse society. Unfortunately, politics and policies persist that continue to divide members of our modern society. Our country's struggle with difference, which initially fell along racial, ethnic, and gender-related lines, has spilled into other areas (i.e., sexual orientation, immigration status, educational achievement, etc.). We have therefore become "comfortably comfortable" with the status quo set by our forefathers and foremothers who thoughtfully yet hypocritically wrote the words "we hold these truths to be self-evident, that all men are created equal." Many would agree that the chasms of conflict and consternation have only deepened since the November 2016 presidential elections.

How do we disrupt this pattern and proclivity toward difference? Empathy may be the key. While empathy is considered critical in medical education, the reality is that it is also lacking (Sulzer, Feinstein, & Wendland, 2016). One study even suggested that empathy may decline in medical school (Hojat et al., 2009). Sulzer et al. performed a systematic review to determine how empathy was conceptualized in medical education research. During their analysis, investigators commented that inconsistencies in defining and operationalizing empathy limited much of the research. This led the authors to conclude that "empathy is relational—an engagement between a subject and an object" (Sulzer et al., 2016, p. 307).

Put simply, contact matters and can create empathy. It is this last point that critically conscious librarians, learners, or leaders should consider when planning educational interventions. Contact facilitates "putting on someone else's shoes" and allows a perspective shift that can only come when one willingly engages in connection and crucial conversations. There is evidence to support that not only do learners desire contact in their training (Gonzalez & Bussey-Jones, 2010) but also contact affects explicit and implicit attitudes (van Ryn et al., 2015).

Any curriculum that desires to improve cultural humility and impact health inequities must include contact. This should occur in small-group settings among community members of similar and disparate backgrounds and also with the very people who are potentially suffering from inequities. Role-playing, panels, case-based discussions, community service, experiential learning activities, patient actors, and real patient interactions should all be considered as crucial components of the ideal longitudinal curricula previously described.

CONCLUSION

The U.S. population is undergoing rapid shifts related to ancestry, ethnicity, and identity. Data suggests that inadequacies in the current American health care system are directly related to inequities occurring for racial and ethnic minorities, as well as other marginalized groups in the United States. As a result, institutions focused on the development of the current and future workforce, not to mention future settings of learning and patient care, must begin to think outside of majority-focused normative behaviors.

Despite valiant efforts to include cultural competency training in medical education settings over the last 20 years, the reality is that many barriers exist to its effective implementation. Unfortunately, bias and insensitivity have been perpetuated by the absence of certain elements, specifically broader sociocultural realities for patients and people and a lack of context related to institutional forces that drive difference.

Since health sciences libraries are crucial components of optimally functioning teaching and research-oriented environments, fully addressing health disparities will require library resources and people adept at engaging with culturally and linguistically diverse members of the training community.

Hopefully, the recommendations herein can serve as a catalyst on the continuum of change that bends toward improving the health and well-being of an increasingly diverse population and workforce.

REFERENCES

Alabi, J. (2015). Racial microaggressions in academic libraries: Results of a survey of minority and non-minority librarians. *Journal of Academic Librarianship, 41*(1), 47–53.

American Library Association. (2012). *Diversity standards: Cultural competency for academic libraries*. Retrieved April 1, 2018, from http://www.ala.org/acrl/standards/diversity

Betancourt, J. R. (2003). Cross-cultural medical education: Conceptual approaches and frameworks for evaluation. *Academic Medicine, 78*(6), 560–569.

Betancourt, J. R. (2006). Cultural competence and medical education: Many names, many perspectives, one goal. *Academic Medicine, 81*(6), 499–501.

Betancourt, J. R., Green, A. R., Carrillo, J. E., & Park, E. R. (2005). Cultural competence and health care disparities: Key perspectives and trends. *Health Affairs, 24*(2), 499–505.

Bullon, A. (2013). Learning by teaching an unsuccessful "cultural sensitivity" course. *Culture, Medicine, and Psychiatry, 37*, 280–287.

Gonzalez, C. M., & Bussey-Jones, J. (2010). Disparities education: What do students want? *Journal of General Internal Medicine, 25*(Suppl. 2), 102–107.

Hawkins, B. W., Morris, M., Nguyen, T., Siegel, J., & Vardell, E. (2017). Advancing the conversation: Next steps for lesbian, gay, bisexual, trans, and queer (LGBTQ) health sciences librarianship. *Journal of the Medical Library Association, 105*(4), 316–327.

Hoffman, K. M., Trawalter, S., Axt, J. R., & Oliver, M. N. (2016). Racial bias in pain assessment and treatment recommendations, and false beliefs about biological differences between Blacks and Whites. *Proceedings of the National Academy of Sciences, 113*(16), 4296–4301.

Hojat, M., Vergare, M. J., Maxwell, K., Herrine, S. K., Isenberg, G. A., Veloski, J., & Gonnella, J. S. (2009). The devil is in the third year: A longitudinal study of erosion of empathy in medical school. *Academic Medicine, 84*(9), 1182–1191.

Kripalani, S., Bussey-Jones, J., Katz, M. G., & Genao, I. (2006). A prescription for cultural competence in medical education. *Journal of General Internal Medicine, 21*(10), 1116–1120.

Kumagai, A. K., & Lypson, M. L. (2009). Beyond cultural competence: Critical consciousness, social justice, and multicultural education. *Academic Medicine, 84*(6), 782–787.

Mestre, L. S. (2010). Librarians working with diverse populations: What impact does cultural competency training have on their efforts? *Journal of Academic Librarianship, 36*(6), 479–488.

Murray-Garcia, J., & Tervalon M. (2017). Rethinking intercultural competence. In D. K. Deardorff & L. A. Arasaratnam-Smith (Eds.), *Intercultural competence in higher education: International approaches, assessment and application* (pp. 19–31). New York: Routledge.

Sue, D. W., Capodilupo, C. M., Torino G. C., Bucceri J. M., Holder, A. M., Nadal, K. L., & Esquilin, M. (2007). Racial microaggressions in everyday life: Implications for clinical practice. *American Psychology, 62*(4), 271–286.

Sulzer, S. H., Feinstein, N. W., & Wendland, C. (2016). Assessing empathy development in medical education: A systematic review. *Medical Education, 50*(3), 300–310.

Tervalon, M., & Murray-Garcia, J. (1998). Cultural humility versus cultural competence: A critical distinction in defining physician training outcomes in multicultural education. *Journal of Health Care for the Poor and Underserved, 9*(2), 117–125.

Tsai, J., Ucik, L., Baldwin, N., Hasslinger, C., & George, P. (2016). Race matters? Examining and rethinking race portrayal in preclinical medical education. *Academic Medicine, 91*(7), 916–920.

U.S. Census Bureau. (2014). Projections of the size and composition of the U.S. population: 2014 to 2060, current population reports (Report No. P25–1143). Retrieved from https://www.census.gov/library/publications/2015/demo/p25-1143.html

van Ryn, M., Hardeman, R., Phelan, S. M., Burgess, D. J., Dovidio, J. F., Herrin, J., & Przedworski, J. M. (2015). Medical school experiences associated with change in implicit racial bias among 3547 students: A medical student CHANGES study report. *Journal of General Internal Medicine, 30*(12), 1748–1756.

Index

About the Editors and Contributors

Shannon D. Jones's (*pronouns: she/her/hers*) career in libraries spans 20 years. Currently, she is the director of libraries for the Medical University of South Carolina in Charleston. In this role, Jones assumes leadership for all aspects of the library, including strategic planning, budgeting, technology integration, facility management and operation, and personnel administration. Prior to her arrival at MUSC, Jones worked as the associate director for research and education at the Tompkins-McCaw Library for the Health Sciences at Virginia Commonwealth University (VCU) in Richmond. Jones received her MLS from North Carolina Central University (NCCU). In addition to the MLS, she also holds a BA in English from North Carolina State University, an MIS from NCCU, and an MEd in adult learning from VCU. Jones is an active member in both the American Library Association and the Medical Library Association, where she is currently serving on the board of directors. Her research interests include staff recruitment and retention, diversity and inclusion in libraries, organizational learning and development, and leadership in academic health sciences libraries.

Beverly Murphy (*pronouns: she/her/hers*) is currently the assistant director for communications and web content management at the Duke University Medical Center Library and Archives, where she manages and maintains the library's website, marketing, and digital communication. She is also the hospital nursing liaison for the Duke Health System, teaching and assisting nurses with their research needs for publication, quality improvement, performance evaluation, and graduate residency. Additionally, she serves as liaison for the students and faculty at the Watts School of Nursing. Murphy has been a librarian for 38 years and is an alumnus of North Carolina Central University in Durham, North Carolina, where she received a BS in biology and an MLS. She is a distinguished member of the Academy of Health Information Professionals and has served in a variety of capacities for the Medical Library Association (MLA), including her current role as the first African American president of the association. Murphy was editor of the *MLA News* for six years and was a member of the *Journal of the Medical Library Association* (*JMLA*) editorial board. She is also active in the Mid-Atlantic Chapter of MLA and the Association of North Carolina Health and Science Libraries (ANCHASL). Her research interests include EHR and OpenInfobutton technology, librarian core competencies, diversity and inclusion in libraries, reference management, and library administration.

* * *

Sonia Alcantara-Antoine, MLS
Pronouns: she/her/hers
Director
Newport News Public Library, Virginia
santoine@nnva.gov

Alan R. Bailey, MLS
Pronouns: he/him/his
Associate professor and head of services, Teaching Resources Center
J. Y. Joyner Library, East Carolina University, Greenville, North Carolina
baileya@ecu.edu

Ene Belleh, MLS, AHIP
Clinical information librarian
Pennsylvania Hospital
University of Pennsylvania Health System, Philadelphia
ene.belleh@uphs.upenn.edu

Chris Bourg, PhD
Pronouns: she/her/hers
Director of libraries
MIT Libraries, Boston
cbourg@mit.edu

Nicole A. Cooke, PhD, MEd, MLS
Pronouns: she/her/hers
Assistant professor
MS/LIS program director
School of Information Sciences
University of Illinois at Urbana–Champaign

nacooke@illinois.edu

Carenado Davis, PhD, MLS
Dean of library services
Wake Technical Community College, Raleigh, North Carolina
cdavis19@waketech.edu

John L. Donovan, PhD
Assistant professor of history
Broward College, Fort Lauderdale, Florida
donovan1959@msn.com

Tristan Ebron, MA
University librarian technician
ECU Laupus Health Sciences Library, East Carolina University, Greenville, North Carolina
MLS student, School of Library and Information Sciences, North Carolina Central University
Ebront14@ecu.edu

Xan Y. Goodman, MLIS
Health sciences librarian and assistant professor
University of Nevada, Las Vegas
xan.goodman@unlv.edu

Rebecca Hankins, MLIS
Pronouns: she/her/hers
Africana resources librarian/curator and associate professor
Cushing Memorial Library and Archives
Texas A&M University Libraries, College Station
rhankins@library.tamu.edu

Amy Kautzman, MLIS
Pronouns: she/her/hers
Dean and director, University Library
California State University, Sacramento
kautzman@csus.edu

kYmberly Keeton, MLS
African American community archivist and librarian
Austin History Center, Austin Public Library, Texas
professorkeeton@gmail.com

Carl Leak, MLS
Pronouns: he/him/his
Health sciences librarian
Health Sciences Library, University Libraries
University of North Carolina, Chapel Hill
celeak@unc.edu

Beth Lesen, PhD
Associate vice president for students affairs/dean of students
California State University, Sacramento
beth.lesen@csus.edu

Brenda Linares, MLIS
Health sciences librarian, School of Nursing
Archie R. Dykes Library
University of Kansas Medical Center, Kansas City
blinares@kumc.edu

Gina Macaluso, MLS, CPM
Pronouns: she/her/hers
Assistant professor/manager, Knowledge River
University of Arizona School of Information Resources and Library
Science, Tucson
ginamacaluso@email.arizona.edu

Tanika Martin, MLS
Youth services manager
Greensboro Public Library, North Carolina
tanika.martin@greensboro-nc.gov

Placedia Miller, MLS
Assistant director
Iredell County Public Library, Statesville, North Carolina
pnance1976@gmail.com

Cheryl Neal
Pronouns: she/her/hers
Library information associate sr.
Delivery, Description, and Acquisitions
University of Arizona Libraries
cneal@email.arizona.edu

Jennifer Nichols, MLIS
Pronouns: she/her/hers
Interim head, Office of Digital Innovation and Stewardship
Digital scholarship librarian
University of Arizona Libraries
jtn@email.arizona.edu

Annabelle V. Nuñez, MA
Pronouns: she/her/hers
Associate director
University of Arizona Health Sciences Library
anunez@email.arizona.edu

Gerald (Jerry) Perry, MLS
Pronouns: he/him/his
Associate dean for health sciences and strategic planning
University of Arizona Libraries, Tucson
jerryperry@email.arizona.edu

JJ Pionke, MA, MSI
Pronouns: he/him/his
Applied health sciences librarian and assistant professor
University Library
University of Illinois–Urbana Champaign
pionke@illinois.edu

Kenyon Railey, MD
Faculty, PA program and assistant chief diversity officer
Office of Diversity and Inclusion, School of Medicine
Duke University, Durham, North Carolina
kenyon.railey@duke.edu

Cristina Dominguez Ramírez, MPA, MSLS, MA
Pronouns: she/her/hers
Library branch manager
Henrico County Public Library, Virginia
cristina.d.ramirez@gmail.com

Ping Situ, BA
Associate librarian
University of Arizona Libraries
psitu@email.arizona.edu

Miriam E. Sweeney, PhD
Pronouns: she/her/hers
Assistant professor
School of Library and Information Studies
University of Alabama, Tuscaloosa
mesweeney1@ua.edu

Shawna Thompson, MLIS
Access and Information Services
Diversity, Social Justice, and Equity Council
University of Arizona Libraries
slt1997@email.arizona.edu

Shaundra Walker, PhD
Pronouns: she/her/hers
Interim library director
Assistant professor of library science
Georgia College, Milledgeville, Georgia
shaundra.walker@gcsu.edu

Janice M. Young, MLS, MEd
Federal librarian
jyoung2988@aol.com